Lyndey Milan

THE BEST COLLECTION
fast, fabulous food

On location filming Christmas with the Australian Women's Weekly.

Sandra Sully, Anna Coren and me—three women from three different commer[cial] networks getting together to publicise the pink ribbon campaign for Breast Cancer charities.

I always enjoy wine tasting.

On the set of At Home with John Mangos, 1993–1995.

Lyndey Milan

THE BEST COLLECTION
fast, fabulous food

NEW HOLLAND

To John,
my companion in all things.

Thanks must go a long way back to those who worked on my first four books, notably Michael Cook, photographer and friend. For this incarnation my gratitude goes to all at New Holland, especially to Managing Director Fiona Schultz for her energy, Lliane Clarke, for her enthusiasm, Hayley Norman for her flair, Ashlea Wallington for her attentiveness, Graeme Gillies for some great shots and my young friend Andrew Ballard for his loyalty and food preparation for all the new recipes.

CONTENTS

Introduction 06

No Plates 08

Small Plates 66

Large Plates 116

Sweet Plates 198

Chocolate Plates 234

Weights & Measurements 268

Index 269

INTRODUCTION

Good food is timeless. If it was really good yesterday, rather than being a fad, then it is good today and will be tomorrow. However, we no longer have the time or perhaps inclination to be in the kitchen which our forbears did. Yet we want to enjoy the same benefits of home cooking, the warm feeling from preparing and sharing food with loved ones. The satisfaction, the joy and the compliments. The good news is we still can.

Fashion comes and goes, but it does leave behind anything good and lasting. So too with cooking ingredients, techniques and styles. It IS possible to progress and embrace the convenience of the modern world, while maintaining the qualities and values of the past. With food, it just takes a bit of a rethink, a welcoming of new flavours and clever use of ingredients.

This is what I wrote in my first book *Plates*, subtitled Real Food For Fast People—the first of the really fast and easy cookbooks. It was an instant hit! *Flavours, A Fresh Approach* followed soon after and then *Lyndey Milan's Fabulous Food* and finally *Balls*, the all round cookbook which I co-authored with Loukie Werle. All were popular and went into several print runs. Obviously they filled a gap in the market.

Fast forward a decade or so and as these books went out of print I was frequently asked for copies. People would email my website, stop me in the street, and others would quote their favourite recipes to me. So I looked at these books carefully again and recalled with joy so many of the recipes. They had stood the test of time, tasted great, were fast and easy to make. The recipes worked. So the idea emerged to package the very best of them together, add some new material and thanks to New Holland, publish a new collection. So here we have it. Choosing which to publish was difficult, they were all so good.

In thinking about the format, we wanted to maintain the difference of my other books, not being bound by a formulaic entrée, main course, dessert model which I find boring. I wanted to reflect how we eat now—maybe no plates, shared plates, or plates of different sizes reflecting contemporary ways of eating. We also thought chocolate deserved a section on its own as it is so perenially popular, and many of these are entirely new recipes.

Moreover, as I am known for my enthusiasm for food and wine matching, and wine being an important part of both *Flavours* and *Fabulous Food*, I have added a wine matching note on every recipe. This is in the form of a stylistic recommendation, rather than a particular wine, so you can follow your own choices there and hopefully learn something of why different wines are best with different foods.

Like any book this has been a labour of love. I have enjoyed cooking the food and tasting the wine. I hope you do too.

Remember, keep cooking and you'll keep smiling!

Lyndey

Catering days with long-time friend Peter Howard. We prepared canapés for a charity dinner where media identities cooked the food.

Christmas with my kids Blair and Lucy.

At a pre-Mother's Day lunch at David Jones with my mum, a good home cook Isabel Hall.

Filming Fresh with the Australian Women's Weekly at Club Med, Lindeman Island.

No Plates

NO PLATES

Pear Confit

Before you make the confit, you will need to poach the pears in wine. Then it is just a matter of boiling and reducing the poaching liquor.

Serves: 6
Preparation time: 10 mins
Cooking time: 30 mins

6 firm medium-sized pears,
preferably a little under-ripe
1 cup (8 fl oz) sugar
2½ cups water
2½ cups white wine
grated rind 1 lemon (optional)
2 teaspoons
lemon juice (optional)
4 cloves (optional)
1 piece cinnamon stick (optional)

To poach the pears:

Peel the pears, leaving them whole, and place with remaining ingredients in a saucepan. Ideally the liquid should just cover the pears. If it doesn't, add more water and wine. Simmer gently for up to 20 minutes, until tender. The key to this recipe is slow poaching—do not plunge the pears into boiling liquid and cook quickly or the flavour will not penetrate.

Remove the pears from the liquid, strain the syrup and pour over them. Serve warm or cold.

To make the confit:

Simply follow the instructions above, omitting the optional ingredients, though perhaps adding a vanilla bean.

After removing the pears, turn up the heat, and boil and reduce the syrup to a caramel consistency. Slice the pears and return to the syrup. Cool. Serve the confit with brie or brioche and mascarpone, or even with ice-cream!

Wine:

The sweetness of the confit demands a sweet wine so a dessert wine is the pick here.

Oranges with Honey and Olive Oil

I came across this dish, which is as surprising as it is simple, in Portugal. It was served by an olive oil producer in a region well known for both honey and olive oil. Just choose varieties with a flavour you love.

Serves: 8
Preparation time: 10 mins
Cooking time: Nil

6 oranges
2 tablespoons honey, approx.
2 tablespoons olive oil, approx.
freshly ground black pepper, optional

Peel oranges, remove pith and slice oranges into rounds. Arrange on a plate and drizzle with honey and olive oil. Sprinkle with pepper, if desired. Serve at the beginning or end of a meal, as a snack, or even as a salad or palate refresher during the meal.

Wine:
As a palate refresher, this is better without wine.

John Mangos and I travelled to Portugal together with the International Olive Oil Council. We had appeared on *At Home with John Mangos* on the Seven Network together for two years.

Watermelon with Iced Gin

I always keep a bottle of gin in the freezer—well, a girl never knows when she might need a martini. It makes a wonderful accompaniment to watermelon. Iced vodka can be substituted and gives a completely different taste sensation.

Watermelon Gin

This is so simple it scarcely needs a recipe. Just cut the watermelon into wedges and serve on a plate beside a shot glass of iced gin. It is imperative that the gin is of a very good quality, such as Tanqueray, Bombay Sapphire or Gordons. Dip watermelon wedges into the gin if you're feeling really decadent.

I met Rick Stein long before he was really famous and we've remained friends. He launched *Fabulous Food* and the watermelon picture was on the cover.

Tomato Tarts
with Fetta and Tapenade

These delightful little finger food items can be made larger to serve as an entree. I use the delicious Persian fetta in olive oil, from Yarra Valley Dairy, but if you can't get this, use goat curd or ricotta.

Makes: 18 tarts
Preparation time: 10 mins
Cooking time: 10–15 mins

2 sheets butter puff pastry
4–6 vine-ripened tomatoes, thinly sliced
2 tablespoons tapenade (see tapenade recipe)
345 g (11 oz) fetta cheese
fresh oregano

Preheat oven to hot, 220°–230°C (430°–450°F, Gas Mark 7). Line a flat baking tray with baking paper. Using a pastry cutter, cut pastry into 6–7cm (2–3in) rounds (you should get 18 rounds). Place on baking paper and prick all over with a fork. Cover with another sheet of baking paper and another oven tray. (This prevents the puff pastry, chosen for its superior flavour, from rising.) Place in oven and cook for 10–15 minutes, or until golden brown. Remove from oven and cool. Just before serving, place a tomato slice on each pastry base, spread with tapenade, top with a small scoop of cheese and garnish with oregano.

Wine:
Choose semillon for a sublime combination with tomato or, if you prefer a red wine, try chambourcin or pinot noir.

Eggplant and Zucchini Fritters

Serves: 10
Preparation time: 10 mins + 30 mins standing
Cooking time: 10 mins

¾ cup plain flour
⅓ cup olive oil
½ teaspoon ground cumin (optional)
2 finger or small eggplants (aubergines),
cut crosswise into 5mm (¼in) slices
3 zucchini (courgettes), cut crosswise into 5mm
(¼in) slices
2 egg whites

Yoghurt Sauce
1 cup natural yoghurt
¼ preserved lemon, rind only, finely chopped
1 clove garlic, crushed
½ tablespoon chopped mint
½ tablespoon chopped flat leaf parsley

Combine flour, oil, cumin if using and 150 ml (5 fl oz) water and beat until smooth.

Sprinkle eggplant and zucchini with salt and stand in a colander for 30 minutes. Pat dry with absorbent paper.

Heat oil in a deep fryer or wok until very hot.

Whisk egg whites until firm peaks form and fold into flour mixture. Dip a few eggplant and zucchini slices at a time in batter and deep-fry in hot oil until crisp. Drain on absorbent paper and serve immediately with yoghurt sauce.

For sauce:
Combine all ingredients and season to taste.

Wine:
Sparkling wine or champagne is very cleansing with anything deep-fried.

Figs in Prosciutto

So simple you do not really require a recipe! It relies on the beautiful flavour of figs in season. The quantities will depend on the size of the figs, so you'll have to estimate.

Makes: 16
Preparation time: 10 mins
Cooking time: Nil

fresh figs
prosciutto

Cut the fresh figs into eighths if they are large. Remove the rind from the prosciutto and cut each slice into three or four pieces, they should be large enough to wrap around a fig segment.

Wine:
A rosé has enough body to handle the prosciutto without overpowering the fig.

In the kitchen with my son Blair.
Both my kids love food and are good cooks.

Tapenade

Provence is the home of this famous olive and caper spread. It takes its name from the French word for capers, but it relies more on olives than capers. Although widely available, it is very easy to make.

Makes: 1 cup
Preparation time: 10 mins
Cooking time: Nil

1 cup (150 g/5 oz) black olives, stoned
pinch of thyme
2 anchovy fillets
1–2 tablespoons capers (depending on personal taste), rinsed
freshly ground black pepper
2 teaspoons lemon juice
2 tablespoons olive oil

Optional extras
1 red chilli, finely chopped
1 tablespoon Continental parsley
pinch of mustard

Combine olives, thyme, anchovies, capers, pepper and any of the optional items in a food processor. Add lemon juice and then slowly add olive oil to make a thick paste. It can be as smooth or as chunky as you like. Keeps well in the refrigerator under a layer of olive oil.

Cook's note:
Tapenade is wonderful spread on bread, Melba toast, bruschetta or focaccia or with anything char-grilled. It also makes a wonderful reduction sauce to serve with veal or beef. Reduce 2 cups (1 pint) beef stock, 1 cup (8 fl oz) wine, ⅓ cup (2¾ fl oz) cream and 1–2 tablespoons tapenade over high heat until sauce is thick.

Wine:
Choose any of the Italian varietals with a tapenade, which is both salty and bitter. This tends to accentuate fruit sweetness in wine. Alternatively, serve a pinot noir, a grenache/shiraz or perhaps a chilled fino sherry.

Spiced Macadamia Nuts

Macadamias, Australia's own native nut, are delicious alone and even more appealing spiced.
As a low-fat option, I've baked them, but they're also great deep-fried.

Makes: 1 small-sized bowl
Preparation time: 5 mins
Cooking time: 10 mins

5 cloves garlic, finely chopped
3 red chillies, sliced, including seeds
extra light olive oil spray
125 g (4 oz) raw macadamia nuts
½ teaspoon ground cumin
2 teaspoons salt
1 teaspoon sugar

Preheat oven to moderate, 180°–190°C (350°–375°F, Gas Mark 4).

Place garlic and chillies in a small, shallow baking tray. Spray lightly with olive oil and toss to coat. Put in oven for 2 minutes. Remove, add macadamias and cumin, spray lightly with oil and shake again. Place in oven for 4 minutes. Remove, shake again and bake for another 4 minutes.

Remove from oven and, while still hot, shake over salt and sugar. Shake again to combine. Cool and store in an airtight container. Delicious to serve with pre-dinner drinks.

Wine:

Try the wonderful nutty, rancio characters of a sherry here, anything from the driest manzanilla and fino to the slightly sweeter oloroso.

Ricotta Balls

These are a terrific, low-fat, vegetarian nibble if you bake them in the oven. Of course, they are also delicious deep-fried.

Makes: 38 balls
Preparation time: 15 mins + chilling time
Cooking time: 3–15 mins

½ cup chopped fresh herbs, e.g. parsley, oregano, basil
¼ cup (1 oz) sun-dried tomatoes and/or sun-dried capsicum
500 g (1 lb) ricotta cheese
100 g (3½ oz) freshly grated parmesan
1½ cups (3½ oz) fresh white breadcrumbs
1 egg
pinch of salt
freshly ground black pepper
¼ cup (1 oz) black olives, about 10, stoned and sliced
60 g (2 oz) polenta

Wine:

Although the flavours are subtle, there is texture here so try a viognier.

Chop herbs finely in a food processor. Add sun-dried tomatoes, ricotta, parmesan, breadcrumbs, egg, salt and pepper and process again, scraping down sides of the bowl once or twice to ensure it is thoroughly mixed. Add olives and process briefly. Refrigerate mixture, if you have time, to firm it and make rolling easier.

Put polenta in a bowl. Roll ricotta mixture into walnut-size balls between your palms. Drop into the polenta. When you have 5 or 6 in the bowl, rotate the bowl to roll the balls around and cover with polenta. Use immediately or rest in refrigerator until required.

Bake in preheated moderately slow oven, 160°C (325°F, Gas Mark 3) for 15 minutes. Alternatively, deep-fry in hot oil, in batches, until golden, about 3 minutes. Drain on crumpled kitchen paper.

Allow to cool just a little before serving, but serve hot.

Cook's note:

You can also bake the ricotta mixture in a 20cm (8in) tin at 160°C (320°F, Gas Mark 3) for an hour.

Labna

Many cuisines have a version of this cheese, which can be eaten any time of day and used in place of fetta in cooking.

Makes: 24
Preparation time: 15 mins + 24 hours draining + 30 mins chilling
Cooking time: Nil

1 litre (2 pints) natural yoghurt
(or low-fat yoghurt)
1 teaspoon salt
extra virgin olive oil
fresh rosemary sprigs
1 teaspoon coriander (cilantro) seeds
2–3 red chillies

Mix yoghurt with salt, stirring well to remove any lumps. Scoop yoghurt into the centre of a double layer of damp muslin and suspend over a deep bowl or plastic container for 24 hours (you may like to scrape the inside of the muslin with a tablespoon a couple of times during the draining period to facilitate draining).

Remove resulting 'cheese' from the muslin and crumble onto a tray lined with paper towels. Refrigerate until firm and dry to the touch. With oiled palms roll into balls about 2.5cm (1in) in diameter. Store in a jar, covered with extra virgin olive oil, with sprigs of rosemary, coriander seeds and red chillies to flavour. Serve on crusty bread with freshly cracked black pepper.

Wine:
Labna has a lovely creamy, yet sour flavour so a wine with lemony acid, like semillon, will work well.

Little Round Sandwiches
with sweet onions, parsley, mayonnaise

Every cocktail party needs some good, simple carbohydrates, and fresh sandwiches are always a winner.

Makes: 20 sandwiches
Preparation time: 15 mins
Cooking time: Nil

1 loaf (about 20 slices) fresh white bread
butter
6 small sweet onions
1 cup (8 fl oz) good quality whole egg
mayonnaise
1 bunch parsley, finely chopped
shredded lettuce (optional)

Using a pastry cutter, cut 2 x 5cm (2in) rounds from each slice of bread. Butter rounds. Slice onions very thinly and sandwich between 2 bread rounds. You may have to remove some of the outer rings to make the onion rounds 'fit' the bread. Spread mayonnaise around the perimeter of the rounds and roll in chopped parsley. Cover with shredded lettuce (to keep moist) and wrap in cling film until ready to serve.

Best eaten within 6 hours.

Wine:
A dry sherry like manzanilla or fino makes a crisp accompaniment or else try a sparkling wine.

On the set of *Fresh* with the *Australian Women's Weekly* on the Nine Network.

Bloody Mary Oyster Shooters

These are terrific at cocktail parties, or as a pre-dinner aperitif and appetizer all in one!

Makes: 24 shooters
Preparation time: 5–10 mins
Cooking time: Nil

150 ml (5 fl oz) vodka or gin
1 tablespoon (1 fl oz) Worcestershire sauce
10 drops Tabasco, or more to taste
½ teaspoon lemon juice
generous salt and freshly ground pepper
1 litre (2 pints) tomato juice
2 dozen oysters

Combine vodka, Worcestershire sauce, Tabasco, lemon juice, salt, pepper and tomato juice and shake with a dozen ice cubes. Drain and pour into shot glasses. Drop an oyster in each and serve immediately.

Cook's note:
Oysters can be bought on the shell, or inexpensively in jars. You can substitute sherry or port glasses for shot glasses.

Wine:
No match here, just drink more shooters!

Oysters with Different Toppings

Oysters must be the most perfect food—and the easiest to serve as they require very little preparation. Pictured are premium-grade Sydney rock oysters and Pacific oysters (the larger ones) on the left.

Makes: 24
Preparation time: 10 mins
Cooking time: Nil

2 dozen oysters
freshly ground black pepper
juice of 1 lime
1 teaspoon Thai sweet chilli sauce
2 tablespoons tomato pasta sauce
2 green onions (shallots), sliced
1 tablespoon fresh ginger julienne
1 tablespoon sweet vinegar seasoning or rice wine vinegar
½ teaspoon sesame oil

Top some of the oysters with freshly ground black pepper and lime juice. Top others with a mixture of Thai sweet chilli sauce and tomato pasta sauce. My favourite combination is a mix of green onion and fresh ginger julienne with Japanese sweet vinegar seasoning and sesame oil.

Wine:
Riesling is a wine that finds echoes in the lime juice can handle the slight chilli and still work with the green onion dressing.

Scallops Steamed with Ginger, Shallots and Sesame

Chinese restaurants serve scallops steamed in this way. I developed this recipe for a seafood class that focussed on seafood and Semillon. It was a winner.

Makes: 24 or serves 4 as an entrée
Preparation time: 10 mins
Cooking time: 2 mins

24 scallops on the shell
2.5cm (1in) knob ginger, finely chopped
3 green onions (shallots), finely chopped
1 tablespoon kecap manis (Indonesian soy sauce) or soy sauce
1 tablespoon water
1 teaspoon sesame oil

Place the scallops (on the shell) in Chinese steamer baskets. Combine the remaining ingredients and spoon over the scallops. Steam over boiling water for about 2 minutes, or until the scallops are opaque and just cooked. Serve immediately.

Wine:
For this dish choose a semillon or serve a chilled fino sherry for a different approach.

Fish Balls with Lemon Grass

These little balls have much more flavour than plain fish and, although they can be served simply as little balls, they look very pretty on the lemon grass 'skewers'.

Makes: 24
Preparation time: 15 mins
Cooking time: 4 mins

315 g (10 oz) green prawns (155 g/5 oz prawn meat)
350 g (11 oz) firm white fish fillets, e.g. gemfish, ling, snapper
1 clove garlic
4 kaffir lime leaves
2 teaspoons Thai red curry paste
1 teaspoon palm (or brown) sugar
salt and pepper, to taste
6 stalks lemon grass
1 tablespoon extra light olive oil or peanut oil
lemon wedges, to serve

Peel prawns and coarsely dice both prawns and fish. Chop garlic and lime leaves in food processor, then add prawns, fish, curry paste, sugar, salt and pepper. Process until combined and still somewhat textured rather than a smooth paste.

Cut each lemon grass stalk into 4 lengths and trim to about 15cm (6in). Mould about 1–2 tablespoons of fish mixture around the end of each lemon grass length. (This can be done several hours in advance; cover with cling film and rest in refrigerator.)

Heat oil in a large non-stick frying pan over medium heat. Cook skewers, turning occasionally, until lightly browned, about 4 minutes. (Alternatively, steam over boiling water—a great way to reduce the fat content.) Serve immediately with lemon wedges.

Wine:
The fruity flavours of a sauvignon blanc will sing with the kaffir lime and lemon grass and soften the heat from the curry paste.

Scallops on the Shell with Asian-Style Vinaigrette

This is a recipe I made up on the spur of the moment. It was 6.30pm and my dinner guests were due in an hour. I wanted something informal to serve with drinks in place of an entree. I had beautiful scallops and just raided my cupboard to come up with something to go with them.

Makes: 36 or serves 6 as an entrée
Preparation time: 10 mins
Cooking time: 2–3 mins

1 clove garlic
2–3 slices fresh ginger
½ cup Continental parsley
2 tablespoons mirin
pinch of rock salt
⅔ cup (5 fl oz) extra virgin olive oil
36 scallops, on the shell

With motor running, drop garlic and ginger into the food processor to chop. Add parsley and, when chopped, add mirin, salt and oil. Process until combined. Spoon over scallops and place under the grill for only a few moments, until scallops are opaque and just warm. Serve immediately.

Wine:
Choose a full-fruited wine as this dressing is rather sweet—chardonnay, riesling or pinot noir would be perfect.

Crab Cakes

Crab meat is now available frozen and often fresh from the fish market. Alternatively, substitute tinned crab.

Makes: 12 or serves 4 as an entrée
Preparation time: 10 mins + mashed potato
Cooking time: 5–10 mins

500 g (1 lb) cooked crab meat
3 green onions (shallots), finely sliced
1 teaspoon grated fresh ginger
1 red chilli, finely chopped
1 tablespoon finely chopped
coriander (cilantro)
1 tablespoon fish sauce
1 teaspoon sugar
mashed potato, made with 440 g (14 oz)
potato, 60 g (2 oz) butter, and ⅓ cup
(2½ fl oz) hot milk
200 g (7 oz) breadcrumbs or desiccated
coconut
1–2 tablespoons peanut oil
fresh coriander leaves or cucumber slices,
to garnish

Combine all ingredients, except breadcrumbs, oil and coriander leaves, and mix well. With wet hands, shape into 12 cakes and roll in breadcrumbs.

Heat oil in non-stick frying pan over high heat and cook crab cakes until golden, about 2 minutes each side. You may need to do this in batches. Drain on paper towel. Serve warm, garnished with a coriander leaf or a thin slice of cucumber, perhaps with a Thai-style cucumber salad.

Wine:
The citrus characters of a crisp dry riesling are the go here, or a herbaceous sauvignon blanc.

Seafood Noodle Balls

Annette Fear, chef at the Spirit House Restaurant and Cooking School at Yandina, near Noosa, cooked these fantastic balls at Sydney's 1998 inaugural Chilli Festival where I matched wines to hot and spicy foods.

Makes: 24 balls
Preparation time: 15 mins
Cooking time: 15 mins

200 g (7 oz) green prawn meat, roughly chopped
200 g (7 oz) squid, roughly chopped
1 red onion, cut in half lengthwise and sliced
½ cup chopped coriander (cilantro) stems
1 tablespoon finely chopped garlic
1 tablespoon finely chopped ginger
2 eggs, beaten
½ cup (2½ oz) plain flour
fish sauce, to season
freshly ground white pepper
1 teaspoon sambal oelek
2 bundles dried egg noodles, soaked in warm water until soft, then drained and cut into 5cm (2in) pieces
vegetable oil, for deep-frying
Thai sweet chilli sauce, to serve

Place all ingredients, except oil, in a large bowl. Mix thoroughly until well combined. Heat oil to a depth of 5cm (2in) in wok or saucepan. Drop teaspoons of mixture into hot oil and cook in batches until golden brown, about 5 minutes. Don't make the balls too large or they will be doughy in the centre. Serve with sweet chilli dipping sauce, if desired.

Wine:
Sparkling wine and champagne can handle spicy food and also cleanse the mouth beautifully between bites of food.

Smoked Salmon and Nori Rolls

Smoked salmon is perennially popular. This is a more modern way of serving it, especially if you use the seaweed that can be purchased at Asian food stores.

Makes: Approx. 20
Preparation time: 15 mins
Cooking time: Nil

a few drips sesame oil
and/or a little chopped dill
250 g (8¾ oz) tub cream cheese
200 g (8 oz) smoked salmon
nori seaweed

Mix the dill or sesame oil (or both) through the cream cheese. Cut the salmon into rectangles (two or three from each slice, depending on size) and put a little of the cream cheese mixture into the middle of each piece. Tuck under the ends and roll to form a neat parcel. Cut seaweed in strips and soak briefly in water. Roll around the middle of each salmon roll.

These rolls will keep for a couple of days in the fridge or, if you really must, they can be frozen.

Wine:
Sparkling wine works well here, especially a rosé or else try a chardonnay.

Polenta Canapés with Prawns

I developed this recipe for an Epicurean Tour, involving a tasting at the Pyrmont store of Simon Johnson, Purveyor of Quality Foods, and finishing at the Sydney Fish Markets for a cooking class using some of the ingredients we had seen. I matched it all with wine. What a day!

Makes: Approx. 30 canapes
Preparation time: 10 mins
Cooking time: 25 mins

2 cups (16 fl oz) water
½ cup (4 oz) polenta (cornmeal)
¼ cup freshly grated parmesan cheese
2 teaspoons chopped fresh basil
2 tablespoons butter, cut into cubes
salt and freshly ground black pepper
20–30 cooked prawns (depending on size), shelled and deveined
2 tablespoons pesto
basil leaves, to garnish (optional)

Bring salted water to the boil. Lower heat to medium and slowly add polenta, whisking as you go. Continue to whisk for up to 10 minutes as the mixture thickens. (You may find it easier to use a wooden spoon.) Continue to cook, stirring occasionally, until the mixture is very thick and comes away from the side of the pan. Add parmesan, basil and butter and season to taste with salt and pepper. Pour into a tray lined with baking paper and refrigerate until set. Using a small pastry cutter, cut into circles (or use a knife to cut into squares or diamonds for less wastage) and reheat in a moderate oven, 180°–190°C (350°–375°F, Gas Mark 4), for 5–10 minutes or on the grill (the grill gives the best texture if you have time). Cut prawns in half, if large, and place on polenta rounds. Top with a little pesto and garnish with basil leaves.

Wine:
Choose a chilled sherry, good-quality sparkling wine or champagne to serve with canapés, otherwise try a chardonnay.

Thai Chicken Balls

When Thai food became popular in Australia, Thai fish cakes were all the rage. This recipe uses chicken instead of fish, while deep-frying keeps it wonderfully moist. To reduce the fat content, they can also be baked.

Makes: 24 balls
Preparation time: 20 mins + optional chilling time
Cooking time: 10 mins

Nam Jim (Sauce)

4 large coriander (cilantro) roots
3 red chillies, seeds removed
15 eschalots, peeled
4 cloves garlic, peeled
155 g (5 oz) palm sugar
¾ cup (6 fl oz)
fresh lime juice (4–5 limes)
2½ tablespoons (1½ fl oz) fish sauce
1 tablespoon chopped coriander leaves, optional

Chicken Balls

1 stalk lemon grass, finely sliced
2 kaffir lime leaves, sliced
2 cloves garlic
3cm (1½in) knob ginger
1 tablespoon Thai red curry paste
2 tablespoons fish sauce
625g (1¼ lb) chicken breast, roughly chopped
1 teaspoon sugar
5 tablespoons coconut cream
Grapeseed, peanut or rice bran oil,
for deep-frying

Make nam jim first. Combine coriander, chilli, eschalots, garlic and sugar in a food processor, then blend in lime juice and fish sauce. Set aside. Stir through coriander leaves if using just before serving.

Heat oil to a depth of 5cm (2in) in deep-sided saucepan over high heat.

Finely chop lemon grass, lime leaves, garlic and ginger in a food processor. Add curry paste and fish sauce and combine. Add chicken and sugar; process until fine, scraping down sides of the bowl at least once. With motor running, add coconut cream and combine well.

As this mixture is rather wet (if you rest it in the refrigerator, it will become a little firmer), roll a teaspoon over and under mixture to form a quenelle shape (egg shape) and drop into hot oil. Cook in batches for about 3 minutes, or until golden brown and cooked through. Remove with a slotted spoon and drain on paper towels. Alternatively, spoon mixture into small non-stick muffin tins, dot a little coconut cream on top and bake in a moderate oven, 180°–190°C (350°–375°F, Gas Mark 4) for 8 minutes. Serve with nam jim.

Wine:

The spicy yet light flavours here are best with a riesling, sauvignon blanc or gewürztraminer.

Thai Salad Wrapped in Lettuce Leaves

Although this may at first appear to be like San choy bau, it is actually quite different. It is served cold and has wonderfully fresh aromatic flavours. It is a version of larb, a cold aromatic minced meat dish from Thailand.

Serves: 12 or 6 as an entrée
Preparation time: 15 mins + cooling time
Cooking time: 7 mins

1 tablespoon peanut oil
500 g (1 lb) chicken breast, finely minced
1 small red onion, finely chopped
⅔ cup chopped coriander (cilantro)
1 tablespoon palm sugar
¼ cup (2 fl oz)
fresh lime juice (3–4 limes)
¼ cup (2 fl oz)
Thai fish sauce (nam pla)
2 tablespoons finely grated ginger
12 small iceberg lettuce leaves

Heat oil over high heat. Add chicken and cook, stirring to break up any lumps, until cooked through, about 6–7 minutes. Remove from heat and place chicken in a bowl to cool.

Add onion and coriander to cooled chicken. Make a dressing by combining palm sugar, lime juice, fish sauce and ginger. (The palm sugar will dissolve in the lime juice.) Add to chicken and mix well.

Blanch the lettuce leaves in boiling water for 1 minute, then refresh under cold water, and drain. Serve each lettuce leaf with a generous scoop of chicken mixture in the centre, wrapping the lettuce loosely around the filling.

Wine:
This is sweet, sour and aromatic so drink a riesling or sauvignon blanc.

Lamb Cutlets with Mint Pesto

Any kind of pesto would be delicious with perfectly cooked, plump, pink lamb cutlets. However, mint and lamb are traditional partners and mint with a hint of chilli is doubly refreshing. These cutlets make ideal finger food.

Serves: 20 (makes 1¼ cups pesto)
Preparation time: 5 mins
Cooking time: 6 mins

20 lamb cutlets
Thai sweet chilli sauce

Mint Pesto
75 g (2½ oz) parmesan cheese
3 cloves garlic
1 bunch fresh mint leaves
pinch of salt
90 g (3 oz) blanched almonds, roasted
(see Cook's note)
1 cup (8 fl oz) olive oil

Brush cutlets with chilli sauce and place under preheated grill for about 3 minutes each side for pink, or cook longer if desired. (Keep a close eye on them as the sugar in the chilli sauce burns easily).

For pesto, grate cheese in a food processor. Remove grating attachment and put in chopping blade. Add garlic and, when chopped, add mint and salt and process to a puree. Add almonds and process to combine. Slowly pour in oil, a little at a time, until pesto is smooth and well combined.

Cook's note:
Roast almonds in a moderate oven, 180°–190°C (350°–375°F, Gas Mark 4), for 5–10 minutes, or microwave on HIGH on a layer of paper towels for 1 minute at a time until golden. Keep any left-over pesto under a layer of olive oil in the fridge and dollop in soups and casseroles.

Wine:
Choose a cabernet sauvignon, many of which have minty characters and so harmonize beautifully with the mint in the pesto.

Potato Roesti
with Seared Beef and Wasabi

Simple and stylish, this idea can be used as finger food with cocktails or as an entrée. Either way it is delicious and easy.

Makes: 22
Preparation time: 10 mins + marinating and resting time
Cooking time: 20 mins

500 g (1 1b) thick piece of rump steak or eye fillet
4 medium to large potatoes, about 850 g (1¾ lb)
60 g (2 oz) butter
250 g (8 oz) crème fraiche
2 teaspoons wasabi
baby rocket (arugula) leaves, to garnish

Marinade

¼ cup (2 fl oz) kecap manis (Indonesian soy sauce) or soy sauce
1 tablespoon honey
1 clove garlic, crushed
1 teaspoon grated ginger
1 teaspoon Chinese five spice powder
1 tablespoon sherry or sake
1 teaspoon sesame oil

Combine marinade ingredients and marinate beef for several hours or overnight, turning occasionally.

Peel and grate potatoes; place in a bowl, and cover with cold water. Melt a little butter in a large pan or electric frypan. Squeeze handfuls of potato dry and fry in small rounds—neaten the shapes by using a 5–6cm (2–2½in) round pastry cutter. Push down with the back of a spoon to compress. (Once each roesti has begun to set and cook, the pastry cutter can be removed and reused for the next roesti.) When golden brown turn over and fry other side until golden. Repeat with remaining butter and potato until all roestis are cooked. Alternatively, once lightly golden on both sides, finish off in a hot oven for 5–10 minutes. Serve warm or at room temperature.

Pan-fry rump at high temperature for only about 2 minutes each side to keep medium rare. (Seal fillet in a pan and cook in a hot oven for 5–10 minutes.) Remove from heat and rest for 10 minutes before slicing.

Top roesti with slices of beef and with a tip of rocket leaf.

Wine:
Wasabi is wonderful with sparkling wine. Choose a rosé style here, to further complement the beef.

Rice Paper Rolls

These are easy to make and different fillings are only limited by your imagination. Rice paper wrappers are available in Asian shops, as are all the ingredients. Traditionally they are filled with barbecued pork or roast duck, but sliced beef or seafood makes a light and delicious change. Make sure you ask for the duck 'not chopped'.

Makes: 40 pieces
Preparation time: 15 mins
Cooking time: Nil

20 rice paper wrappers
½ Chinese roast duck or barbecued pork, sliced
2 Lebanese cucumbers, shaved into fine slices or thin wedges
snow pea shoots
bean shoots
½ cup hoisin or char siew sauce

To use the wrappers, simply soak them, one at a time, for a minute or two in warm water so they become pliable. Lay flat on a clean dry tea towel and fill with a slice of duck or pork, Lebanese cucumber, snow pea shoots, bean shoots and a teaspoon of hoisin or char siew sauce. Fold in the ends, roll up the wrapper and roll it over the filling to form a cylinder. Cut on the diagonal into two pieces.

Wine:
The fuller flavours of these meats are best matched with a rose champagne or sparkling wine or even a sherry as an aperitif. Otherwise pinot noir makes a classic match with duck.

Easy San Choy Bau

A long-time favourite in my household. My kids called it 'Chinese hamburger' when they were growing up.

Serves: 4
Preparation time: 10 mins
Cooking time: 12 mins

crisp iceberg lettuce
2 tablespoons oil
750 g (1½ lb) lean pork mince
1 small cup water chestnuts, drained and chopped
4 slices fresh ginger, peeled and chopped
¼ cup (2 fl oz) chilli sauce
2 tablespoons dry sherry
1 tablespoon soy sauce
1 teaspoon sugar
salt and pepper to taste
2 tablespoons cornflour
½ cup (4 fl oz) chicken or beef stock

Carefully separate lettuce leaves and trim with scissors to form neat cups. Place in iced water to crisp.

Heat a wok or fry pan and add the oil. Stir-fry the pork, chestnuts and ginger in the oil until the meat is no longer pink. Stir in the chilli sauce, sherry, soy sauce, sugar, salt and pepper.

Blend the cornflour and stock together and add this mixture to the wok or pan. Cook for a further 1–2 minutes, stirring.

Place the drained cupped lettuce leaves on a serving plate and fill each leaf with 3–4 tablespoons of the warm stir-fried mixture. Roll up the leaves and serve.

Wine:
Rosé has a depth of flavour to carry these flavours.

Pork Dim Sims

I came up with this recipe when looking for something to cook for Chinese New Year. Traditionally, these dim sims would be deep-fried after steaming but, ever mindful of the needless addition of fat, I prefer to serve them steamed. The flavour is better too!

Makes: 20–30
Preparation time: 15 mins
Cooking time: 7–8 mins

50 g (1¾ oz) bamboo shoots, drained
3 eshallots or 1 medium onion, sliced
1 bunch garlic chives, chopped (optional)
500 g (1 lb) finely minced lean pork
1 packet wonton wrappers

Seasoning
2 teaspoons soy sauce
2 teaspoons dry sherry
1 teaspoon salt
2 teaspoons sugar
¼ teaspoon black pepper
2 teaspoons sesame oil
1 tablespoon cornflour

Finely dice the bamboo shoots, eshallots and garlic chives (if you are using them) in a food processor. Add pork and blend until smooth. Add seasoning ingredients and mix well.

Place a generous spoonful of this mixture in the centre of each wonton wrapper and pull up the sides to make dumplings, the pastry should nearly reach the top of each one.

Arrange the dim sims in large greased bamboo steaming baskets and steam over high heat, covered, for 7–8 minutes.

Simply serve direct from the steamer with a little bowl of sweet chilli sauce.

Wine:
The crisp, dry flavours of a sherry complement these flavours or else try a pinot gris or viognier.

Pasta Shells with Tomato, Basil and Tapenade

These are a surprisingly inexpensive and easy finger food.

Makes: 20 shells
Preparation time: 10–15 minutes
Cooking time: 10 minutes

20 very big pasta shells
10 small or 5 large cherry tomatoes
1 tablespoon tapenade (see tapenade recipe)
50 g (1¾ oz) marinated fetta
baby basil leaves

Cook pasta shells in plenty of salted boiling water. Drain and run under cold water until cool. Drain well.

Cut cherry tomatoes in half if they are small or quarters if they are large. Arrange pasta shells on serving platter. Place a dollop of tapenade in the bottom of each pasta shell. Push in a cherry tomato portion, a little fetta and top with a baby basil leaf. If baby basil is not available, shred larger basil leaves. These will store in the fridge for a few hours. Serve as finger food.

Chef's note:
Buy the biggest size pasta shells you can. Conchiglie Rigate are the size most readily available. Sometimes giant pasta shells, Conchiglioni Rigati are available and can be stuffed with many more, or larger ingredients.

Wine:
Try a young semillon with the fresh flavours of this dish.

Our first big catering function, preparing the entrée for a charity fundraiser. I am 9th from the left.

On location shooting a Christmas Special with Peter Everett.

In the kitchen with my daughter Lucy.

Small Plates

SMALL PLATES

Aromatic Vegetables

The ideal accompaniment to any dish or simply to enjoy on its own.

Serves: 4 or 6 as a side dish
Preparation time: 10 mins
Cooking time: 8 mins

3 medium carrots, diced
3 medium zucchini (courgettes), cubed
¾ cup (8 oz) peas
20 snow peas (mangetout), sliced
100 ml (3½ fl oz) cream
250 g (8 oz) butter
extra butter for sautéing
1 small leek, sliced
½ tablespoon each of chopped thyme, chives, basil, chervil and tarragon
salt

Blanch the vegetables (except the leek) in boiling water and refresh under cold water. Set aside.

Reduce the cream until it is just thick. Whisk in the butter. Set aside.

Heat a little butter in a pan. Lightly sauté the leek and then the blanched vegetables. Reduce the heat and add the cream/butter sauce. Sprinkle generously with chopped herbs. Season to taste and serve immediately.

Wine:

If enjoying this as a side dish, chose a wine to match the main course. To eat solo, try the rich, rounded flavours of chardonnay.

Green Pawpaw Salad

My version is inspired by a very popular Thai recipe. The pawpaw must be very green—if your fruiterer doesn't regularly stock them, order one in. To serve as a light meal, add 250 g (8 oz) small prawns or shredded chicken and roasted peanuts at the last minute.

Serves: 6–8 as an accompaniment
Preparation time: 10 mins
Cooking time: Nil

1 medium green pawpaw (papaya), about 750 g (1½ lb)
1 clove garlic, finely chopped
2.5cm (1in) piece ginger, grated
2 spring onions, finely sliced
1 red or green chilli, seeded and chopped
¼ cup (2 fl oz) lime juice (from 1–2 limes)
2 tablespoons Thai fish sauce
1 tablespoon palm sugar (or brown sugar)

Peel, seed and julienne pawpaw. (A Japanese grater does an excellent job, or shave with a vegetable peeler and cut into long fine strips.) Mix with garlic, ginger, spring onion and chilli.

Combine remaining ingredients, stirring until sugar has dissolved, and pour over pawpaw mixture.

Wine:
The acid in this dish makes matching a wine difficult. Try a sauvignon blanc.

Asparagus on Garlicky Bean Puree with Crisp Pancetta

Asparagus is the most wonderful vegetable. To prepare, simply bend at the end and it will snap off in exactly the right place. Beans and pulses are very good for us and we don't use them often enough—pureed they are wonderful with all sorts of things.

Serves: 4
Preparation time: 5 mins
Cooking time: 10 mins

1 tablespoon butter
2 cloves garlic
310 g (10 oz) canned white beans e.g. cannelini, butter beans
4 slices pancetta
2 bunches asparagus
extra virgin olive oil

Melt butter in a small saucepan and cook garlic gently over low heat. Add beans, including their liquid (see Cook's note), and heat through. Mash or puree in food processor. Grill or dry-fry pancetta in a non-stick pan.

Meanwhile, bring plenty of water to the boil in a frying-pan or asparagus steamer and cook asparagus for a few minutes, or until cooked but still firm. (You could also use your microwave.) Drain.

To serve, place some bean puree on 4 plates, top with asparagus, crisp pancetta and a drizzle of olive oil.

Cook's note:
Taste the liquid in the canned beans—sometimes it has food acid in it which is not very palatable. If so, drain and rinse beans and substitute water or stock for the liquid.

Wine:
Choose the classic wine to serve with asparagus—sauvignon blanc—to highlight its crisp herbaceousness.

Chilled Minted Pea and Lettuce Soup

This is a revival of an old classic, as good now as it was years ago. It also makes a lovely hot soup.

Serves: 8
Preparation time: 5 mins + chilling
Cooking time: 25 mins

1 iceberg or cos lettuce, washed
500 g (1 lb) frozen baby peas or shelled, fresh peas
1 litre (2 pints) chicken stock
1 cup (10 oz) thick European-style yoghurt
2 tablespoons finely chopped mint
or small mint leaves, to serve (optional)

Break up lettuce and place in a large saucepan with peas and chicken stock. Cover and place over high heat until it comes to the boil (around 10–15 minutes). Simmer until peas are tender, around 10 minutes more. Remove from heat and cool a little.

Process in food processor or blender for a finer texture. Stir in yoghurt and mint if you are using it. Chill in the fridge for at least an hour prior to serving.

Great with crusty bread or cornmeal muffins.

Cook's note:
To serve hot, return to the boil after pureeing and then stir in yoghurt a spoon at a time and serve immediately. Do not reboil or yoghurt may curdle.

Wine:
Choose a soft, approachable white wine like a marsanne, viognier, colombard or chenin blanc.

I have been cooking at the Sydney Royal Easter Show for over 20 years. Here I am in 2007.

Pear Vichyssoise with Spinach

Vichyssoise, or potato and leek soup, is a classic which can be served hot or cold. Here the addition of pear gives it a lightness while the spinach contributes freshness.

Serves 8–10
Preparation time: 10 mins
Cooking time: 35 mins

2 large leeks, cleaned and halved
1 small onion
50 g (1¾ oz) butter
5 medium potatoes, approx 800 g (1¾ lb)
1 litre (4 cups) chicken stock
salt to taste
825 g (1¾ lb) tin pears in natural juice
1 cup (8 fl oz) cream
freshly ground black pepper
1 small bunch (or ½ large) English spinach, leaves only, washed

Slice white part of leeks and onion and fry gently in the butter until just turning golden, around 6–8 minutes. Add the peeled and sliced potatoes, chicken stock and. Bring to the boil, reduce heat and simmer gently for about 20 minutes or until potatoes are soft.

Meanwhile, drain the tin of pears, reserving the juice. Set at least four good halves aside and slice neatly.

Blend remaining pears and juice with the cooked vegetable mixture until smooth in food processor or blender. You will need to do this in batches. Add cream and pepper to taste. Return to the rinsed out saucepan and bring again to simmering point. Thin with water if desired.

Stack spinach leaves on top of each other, roll over tightly in a cigar shape and slice finely—this is called a chiffonnade. Stir into soup. Remove from heat and either serve immediately or chill. Taste again to check seasoning as cold foods require more seasoning than hot.

Ladle into bowls. Garnish with sliced pear and an extra grind of black pepper. Serve with crusty bread.

Cook's note:
This makes a lot of soup—you could halve the recipe but I think it's worth making a lot.

Wine:
Sublime with a young, elegant chardonnay.

Pumpkin and Coconut Soup

Pumpkin soup is a perennial favourite in Australia. Here it is given an Asian twist with the addition of spice and coconut. Orange sweet potato can be substituted for the pumpkin, but it gives a thicker puree so you will need to add a little more stock.

Serves: 4 as a main or 6 as an entrée
Preparation time: 10 mins
Cooking time: 20 mins

1 small or ½ large butternut pumpkin, just over 1 kg (2 lb) unpeeled
1 tablespoon olive oil
1 onion, chopped
1 teaspoon or more freshly grated ginger
1 teaspoon coriander (cilantro) seeds
1½ cups (12 fl oz) chicken or vegetable stock
1½ cups (12 fl oz) coconut milk
salt and freshly ground pepper
2 teaspoons lemon juice
½ bunch fresh coriander

Peel and seed pumpkin and cut into chunks. Heat a frying pan with some olive oil and cook onion, without browning, until softened. Increase heat and add ginger and coriander seeds. Add pumpkin, turning to coat in oil (about 1 minute). Add stock, cover pan and simmer for 10 minutes, or until pumpkin is soft. Puree contents of pan in a food processor, gradually adding coconut milk. Season to taste with salt, pepper and lemon juice.

To serve, ladle into bowls and sprinkle with fresh coriander leaves.

Wine:
Serve with chilled sherry, or try a blended white wine, such as a semillon/chardonnay, semillon/sauvignon blanc or classic dry white three-blend style.

Roasted Tomato and Orange Soup

I find roasting vegetables before making a soup or sauce intensifies their flavour. It's a lovely technique if you have time.

Serves: 4
Preparation time: 10 mins
Cooking time: 30–40 mins

1 tablespoon olive oil
750 g (1½ lb) ripe tomatoes, quartered
1 red onion, peeled and quartered
3 cloves garlic, peeled
1 carrot, peeled and chopped
2 teaspoons sugar
salt and freshly ground black pepper
juice and zest of 1 large of 2 small oranges
375 ml (13 fl oz) chicken stock
a few fresh basil leaves, torn if large
char-grilled or crusty bread to serve, optional

Preheat oven to 200°C (400°F, Gas Mark 6).

Pour olive oil into baking dish. Add tomatoes, onion, garlic and carrot. Sprinkle with sugar, salt and pepper. Toss all together. Roast for 30–40 minutes or until vegetables are soft and the edges are beginning to blacken.

Whiz together in food processor or blender. Blend in orange juice, zest and chicken stock. Pour into a large saucepan and heat. (If you want to serve cold, refrigerate at this point.) Taste and adjust seasoning if necessary. Ladle into serving bowls and scatter with fresh basil leaves. Serve with bread of choice.

Cook's note:

If tomatoes are not in season and the soup is not tomatoey enough, add a tablespoon of tomato paste.

Wine:

Semillon is always a good match for tomatoes as both have significant acid.

Michael's Mushroom Risotto

A recipe from Michael Cook, who photographed my first three books. I can't believe that something so simple and that goes against all the accepted rules could taste so good! I find any pungent European (not Chinese) dried mushrooms, such as boletus or cèpes, work equally well. No need to soak them first.

Serves: 3
Preparation time: 5 mins
Cooking time: 20 mins + 5 mins standing

1 cup (8 oz) arborio rice
3 cups (1½ pints) water
10–20 g (⅓–⅔ oz) dried porcini mushrooms, crumbled coarsely
1 tablespoon (⅔ fl oz) olive oil
salt and pepper
1–1½ teaspoons Vecon vegetable extract or good quality powder like Massel
1 tablespoon olive oil (extra) or butter
freshly grated Parmesan cheese

Simply place everything except the Parmesan cheese and extra oil or butter in a very large microwave-safe container with a firmly fitting lid. Cook on HIGH for 20 minutes. Remove from the microwave and stir, there should still be some liquid left. Allow to stand 5 minutes or so to complete the cooking and absorb the liquid. Add another good slosh of olive oil (or butter to be more traditional), mix through and serve with freshly grated Parmesan cheese.

Wine:
The funky flavours of the porcini are miraculous with pinot noir.

Wild Mushroom Pasta

I just love the many varieties of mushroom and fungi now available fresh. This is a basic recipe for a mushroom ragout that can be served in a little pot or ramekin with crusty bread as an entree, or with meat or pasta as a main course.

Serves: 6 as an entrée, 4 as a main course
Preparation time: 10 mins
Cooking time: 12 mins

500 g (1 lb) rigatoni
125 g (4 oz) black fungus
125 g (4 oz) button mushrooms
125 g (4 oz) shiitake mushrooms
155 g (5 oz) shimeji mushrooms
90 g (3 oz) butter
1 onion, chopped
1 clove garlic, crushed
1¼ cups (10 fl oz) cream
¾ cup (6 fl oz) chicken or vegetable stock
salt and freshly ground pepper
125 g (4 oz) enoki mushrooms
½ bunch garlic chives, with flowers, if in season

Bring 4 litres salted water to a rolling boil. Add rigatoni and cook following directions on packet. Wipe mushrooms clean with a kitchen towel or soft cloth and slice, leaving some small mushrooms whole for variety. Melt all but 1 tablespoon butter in a frying pan over medium heat. Soften the onion, adding garlic after 1–2 minutes. When onion is wilted but not brown, add all the mushrooms, except the enoki. Cook until almost cooked through, then stir in cream and stock. Bring to the boil and simmer. Season with salt and pepper to taste. Cook enoki mushrooms in remaining butter in a separate pan.

Drain pasta and put into a large warmed bowl. Pour the sauce over and toss pasta through. The sauce will cook more as it clings to the hot pasta. Garnish with enoki mushrooms and snip garlic chives over the top.

Wine:
Choose a flavoursome wine, such as chardonnay, with rich, creamy foods or for red wine lovers, pinot noir is wondrous with mushrooms.

Mushrooms En Brioche

Buy individual brioche from your patisserie, allowing one per person. For the ragout, select a variety of fresh mushrooms; preferably at least three of the following: shiitake, field, Swiss brown, enoki, oyster, cup or button.

Serves: 8
Preparation time: 5 mins
Cooking time: 15 mins

1 kg (2 lb) mixed mushrooms
butter
100 ml (3½ fl oz) beef stock or wine
1¼ cups (10 fl oz) thickened cream
salt and freshly ground black pepper
8 individual brioche

Wipe the mushrooms clean with some paper towelling or a soft cloth. Slice the larger mushrooms, leaving the small mushrooms whole for variety. Sauté them in butter in a frypan. Stir in a little beef stock or wine, cream, season with salt and pepper and bring to the boil, simmering until it is reduced and slightly thickened.

Meanwhile, remove the bump on top of the brioche and scoop out a little of the filling. Place them in the oven to warm while the ragout thickens.

Remove brioche from oven. Spoon some of the filling into each brioche, allowing it to spill over the edge onto the plate. Replace the lid.

Wine:
Pinot noir often has a funky, mushroomy character and so makes a great match. For white wine lovers, chardonnay clears the palate in between mouthfuls.

Dry Portuguese Prawn Soup

Serves: 6–8
Preparation time: 20 mins
Cooking time: 35–45 mins

1 kg (2 lb) small to medium green prawns
60 g (2 oz) butter
1.5 litres (3 pints) fish stock
½ cup (4 fl oz) white wine or rose
2 fresh bay leaves
few sprigs flat leaf parsley
few sprigs coriander (cilantro)
2 ripe red tomatoes, roughly chopped
¼ cup olive oil
2 onions, chopped
5 cloves garlic, minced
2–3 red chillies, deseeded and finely chopped
one day old loaf of broa (Portuguese bread),
small French stick or Italian rolls
¼ cup extra virgin olive oil
sea salt
freshly ground black pepper
3 or more eggs to taste, at room temperature
½ cup coarsely chopped fresh coriander

Shell and devein prawns. Melt butter in a large saucepan and add prawn heads and shells and saute, stirring frequently until coloured. Cover with fish stock and wine, add bay leaves, parsley, coriander and tomatoes and bring to the boil. Simmer for at least 20–30 minutes.

Meanwhile heat olive oil in a heavy based pan. Stir-fry onions, adding 4 cloves garlic and chilli after a couple of minutes. Cook until soft and golden. Remove from heat.

Pre-heat oven to 200°C (400°F, Gas Mark 6).

Break the bread into small chunks and place in a large soup tureen. Sprinkle over remaining garlic clove. Drizzle with extra virgin olive oil. Toss. Place soup tureen in a hot oven while you complete the soup.

Strain prawn stock through a colander, pressing down firmly with a potato masher to extract all the juices. Return to the heat. When the stock is at a rolling boil, season to taste and drop in the prawns and cook for 2–3 minutes. Remove some of the prawns for garnish. Add the onion mixture to the soup and stir well. Return to the boil.

Pour the boiling hot prawn mixture into the hot soup tureen, on top of the bread. Stir to combine a little. Break the eggs into the top, spacing them apart. Scatter with the coriander and garnish with reserved prawns.

Rush the acorda to the table. To serve, stir the eggs, prawns and coriander down into the mixture and ladle into large heated soup plates.

Wine:
A rosé is wonderful with this as it has more body than a white wine which suits these robust flavours.

Prawns Poached in Lemon Grass Broth

This recipe is based on one from Brisbane Masterclass, an annual weekend gourmet gab fest, but I serve it hot, not cold as originally intended.

Serves: 4–6
Preparation time: 10 mins
Cooking time: 10 mins

1 litre (2 pints) chicken consomme or clear chicken stock
2 stems lemon grass, sliced into rounds
4 kaffir lime leaves
8 black peppercorns
1 sprig of mint
24 green medium king prawns, peeled and deveined

Bring stock to the boil with all the flavouring ingredients, except prawns. Reduce heat to a simmer and add prawns. Poach for 2–3 minutes, or until prawns are just cooked through and opaque. Serve immediately in bowls with some of the broth.

Wine:
Choose a semillon for a sensational pairing.

I spent nearly nine years as Food Director of *The Australian Women's Weekly.* This photo was taken at the 70th birthday celebration for the magazine on the TV show *This is Your Life.*

Prawn Soup

Every time I shell prawns I freeze the shells in little packets in the freezer. When I have about half a kilo in wieght of prawn shells, I make this recipe. It is very economical as it needs no fresh prawns.

Serves: 8
Preparation time: 5 mins
Cooking time: 70 mins

125 g (4 oz) butter
500 g (1 lb) prawn shells and heads
2 leeks, cleaned and sliced
1 sprig tarragon
1 carrot, peeled and sliced
4 large red tomatoes, chopped
1 litre white wine
1 slice white bread
2 tablespoons rice
1 litre cream
salt and pepper to taste

Melt the butter in a large saucepan or stockpot and fry the prawn heads and shells until they are opaque but not brown. Add the rest of the ingredients, bring to the boil and simmer slowly for an hour until the vegetables are cooked. Give the mixture a good mashing with a potato masher to help extract the flavours. Strain through a sieve leaving only a fairly dry residue.

Serve as it is, or put one shelled prawn per person in each bowl just for show. You don't need it for flavour!

Wine:
This is such a full-bodied and rich soup, it can handle a full-bodied chardonnay or try the classic match of a sherry.

Seafood Ravioli

I love this recipe. Seafood ravioli are so terribly glamorous yet, using wonton skins, so easy to create. They have a silky texture, just like good hand-made pasta. You will need to allow at least two ravioli per person and each ravioli takes two wonton skins.

Serves: 4–6
Preparation time: 10 mins
Cooking time: 10 mins

1 cup (8 fl oz) fish stock
150 ml (5 fl oz) cream
splash of white wine (optional)
24 wonton skins
a little milk
selection of seafood, such as 1 prawn, 1 scallop and 1 small cube of fish per ravioli
chopped fresh herbs

To make the sauce, reduce the fish stock, cream and wine (if you are using it) until thickened.

Lay out wonton skins on a flat surface. Paint the edges with a little milk using a pastry brush or your finger. Place your selection of seafood, I suggest a prawn, a scallop and some fish on top of each wonton skin. Cover with another wonton skin and squeeze together around the circumference to join.

Cook briefly in salted boiling water. Add chopped fresh herbs to the sauce. Place the individual servings of ravioli in bowls and top with the sauce. Eat and enjoy!

Wine:
There are soft, creamy yet delicate flavours here so try a lean, elegant chardonnay from a cool climate region.

Spicy Thai Prawns

Thai food is based on a balance of hot, sweet, sour and salty. These flavour components can be adjusted according to taste.

Serves: 4
Preparation time: 10 mins
Cooking time: 10 mins

1 tablespoon oil
1–3 fresh red or green chillies to taste
2 onions, chopped
6 tablespoons chopped garlic
1 tablespoon minced ginger
2 tablespoons chopped coriander root (from one bunch of coriander/cilantro)
400 g (14 oz) shelled green prawns
½ bunch green onions (shallots), finely chopped
2 tablespoons sugar
1 teaspoon salt
4 tablespoons lemon juice
4 tablespoons Thai fish sauce (nam pla)
chopped fresh coriander

Heat oil in pan or wok and sauté the chillies, onions, garlic, ginger and coriander root until the onion is transparent but not brown. Add prawns and green onions and continue to cook until prawns are opaque and almost cooked. Sprinkle over sugar and salt, then add lemon juice and fish sauce. Taste and adjust the spiciness with chillies, sweetness with sugar, sourness with lemon juice and saltiness with salt or fish sauce.

Serve with the coriander sprinkled over the top.

Wine:

Lots of heat and spice here, so try a riesling, gewürztraminer or sauvignon blanc.

Spirelli with Crab and Lemon

Use spirelli or spiral pasta for this dish as the sauce clings to it beautifully. Fresh crab meat is sometimes available from your fishmonger, so order it to save having to get it from a crab yourself.

Serves: 2
Preparation time: 5 mins
Cooking time: 12 mins

150 g (5 oz) spirelli pasta
1¼ cups (10 fl oz) pure cream
zest of 1 lemon
100 g (3½ oz) fresh crab meat
salt and pepper

Cook the pasta in plenty of salted, boiling water. When it is almost cooked, simply heat the cream with the zest of a lemon. Then stir in the crab meat, return to the boil and season with salt and pepper. Serve immediately over the hot, drained pasta. If you prefer to use less cream, replace some of it with fish stock.

Cook's note:
Allow around 75 g (2⅔ oz) raw pasta per person.

Wine:
The flavours here are lemony and creamy, so try a chardonnay or else an aged Semillon with honeyed toasty characters.

Chicken Kofta

These light chicken balls are a real winner as finger food, an entree or main. Delicious alone as a finger food, they are also good with a simple sauce made of tomato pasta sauce, freshly chopped garlic and coriander and a little extra virgin olive oil.

Serves: 4
Preparation time: 15 mins + 30 mins chilling
Cooking time: 5 mins

¼ bunch flat-leaf parsley
¼ bunch coriander (cilantro)
4 thick slices stale white bread, crusts removed
75 g (2½ oz) shelled, unsalted, roasted pistachios
2 teaspoons ground cumin seeds
¼ teaspoon chilli flakes
juice of 1 lemon
1 double chicken breast, about 470 g (15 oz), roughly chopped
90 g (3 oz) sesame seeds (or couscous)
1–2 tablespoons olive oil, for shallow-frying
tomato sauce, to serve
couscous, to serve

With food processor motor running continuously, chop herbs, then add bread. When fine crumbs form, add pistachios and pulse until coarsely chopped. Add spices, lemon juice and chicken meat and blend only until combined. Season to taste and mix again, if necessary.

With damp hands roll mixture into walnut-size balls. Roll in sesame seeds or couscous to coat and refrigerate for 30 minutes. Heat olive oil and cook kofta, shaking pan frequently to roll kofta, for 5 minutes, or until evenly golden brown and cooked through. Drain on paper towels and serve warm with tomato sauce and couscous.

Cook's note:
Make your own tomato sauce or use a good bottled pasta sauce.

Wine:
Drink a light red wine such as chambourcin or sangiovese.

Chicken and Sweetcorn Soup

This is an incredibly simple version of the Chinese classic.

Serves: 4–6
Preparation time: 5 mins
Cooking time: 10 mins

1 litre (2 pints) chicken stock
2 tablespoons sherry or Chinese cooking wine
1 tablespoon grated ginger
1 clove garlic, crushed
1 tablespoon light soy sauce
420 g (15 oz) can creamed corn
1 small chicken breast, sliced
2 pinches white pepper
1 egg, beaten
6 green onions (shallots) chopped

Bring chicken stock, sherry, ginger, garlic and soy sauce to the boil in a large saucepan over medium high heat. Reduce heat and simmer 3 minutes.

Add creamed corn and chicken return to the boil then simmer 3 more minutes or until chicken is cooked through. Add white pepper and salt if desired.

With the soup boiling, slowly whisk egg into this so it forms small threads.

Lade into individual serving bowls and scatter with green onions.

Wine:
Try a sherry, especially if you are cooking with one in this soup.

Chicken Consommé with Angel Hair

Angela hair or Capelli d'Angelo is very fine pasta, also called vermicelli, available both fresh and dried. It is made from eggs so don't confuse it with rice or mung bean vermicelli which is an Asian ingredient.

Serves: 4–6
Preparation time: 5–10 mins
Cooking time: 5–10 mins

salt
125 g (5 bundles/4 oz) angel hair pasta or vermicelli
1 litre (2 pints) chicken consomme
1 carrot, approx 150 g (5 oz), peeled and cut into thin sticks
1 bunch fine asparagus, cut into 2cm (1in) pieces
150 g (5 oz) snowpeas (mangetout), topped and tailed, sliced diagonally
white pepper

Bring plenty of salted water to the boil and cook pasta until soft and strands unwind, around 5 minutes. Drain, separating any pasta which has stuck together under a running tap.

Meanwhile bring chicken consommé and 750 ml (1½ pints) water to the boil in a large saucepan. Add carrot, asparagus stems (but not tips) and return to the boil and simmer 2 minutes. Add asparagus tips and snow peas, return to the boil and cook for a minute or two or until vegetables are soft. Season to taste.

Place a pile of pasta in bowls and top with vegetables and soup.

Cook's note:
Chicken consommé is available in both tetra packs and tins in the stock or soup section of the supermarket. Vegetarians may prefer to use vegetable stock but either make your own or water down a commercial one as they can be very strong.

Wine:
A light, delicate dish so try a marsanne or chenin blanc.

Asian-Scented Broth with Chicken Wontons

Another deceptively simple dish to create, yet it looks and tastes sensational.

Serves: 6
Preparation time: 10 mins
Cooking time: 10 mins

4 cups (2 pints) chicken stock or consommé
2 teaspoons kecap manis
(Indonesian sweet soy sauce)
2 tablespoons mirin
2 large green onions (shallots) cut into 3cm (1in) pieces
½ fresh chilli
1 stalk coriander (cilantro)
1 chicken breast
salt
12 wonton skins
1 tablespoon milk
1 cup (8 fl oz) extra stock or salted water
coriander leaves and chilli for garnish

Wine:
Often soup doesn't really need a wine, though a small glass of dry sherry works well.

Combine the stock, kecap manis, mirin and green onions in a saucepan and bring to the boil.

Meanwhile combine the chilli, coriander (if you like it), chicken breast and salt in the food processor and process until well mixed. You can leave it with a coarse texture or process to a smooth paste.

Bring the extra stock or water to the boil.

Lay the wonton skins flat and brush the edges with milk. Place ½ teaspoon of the mixture in the centre of each skin. Fold over and press together with your fingers to form a neat semi-circle.

Drop each wonton into the simmering stock or water and cook until they float. They cook very quickly, in a matter of moments. Don't cook them in the chicken soup as it will turn cloudy.

Remove the wontons and place in bowls. Top them with the simmering soup. Garnish with coriander leaves and, perhaps, some fine slices of chilli.

Duck Soup with Coriander and Noodles

Serves: 6
Preparation time: 5–10 mins
Cooking time: 20 mins

1 whole Chinese roasted duck
3 sticks lemongrass
1 bunch coriander (cilantro), roots and leaves
2 litres (4 pints) chicken stock or water
5cm (2in) root ginger, peeled and chopped
6 fresh kaffir lime leaves, bruised
1 star anise
6 bunches Asian greens e.g. baby bok choy, washed and roughly chopped
1 tablespoon fish sauce
1 teaspoon sesame oil
600 g (1⅓ lb) thin egg noodles
½ bunch green onions (shallots)

Pre-heat oven to 170°C (300°F, Gas Mark 3).

Take the duck meat off the bone and set aside. Roughly chop carcass and put in a large saucepan. Peel lemon grass and chop only the white part near the root end and then crush slightly with the side of the knife. Finely chop coriander root. Place in saucepan with the chicken stock or water, duck bones, ginger, lime leaves and star anise and simmer over medium heat for 15 mins.

Meanwhile place duck meat skin side up on a baking sheet and roast for 15 minutes or until hot, golden and the fat has run out. Drain on kitchen towel and cut meat on a diagonal into 2–3cm (1in) strips. Keep warm.

Strain stock into a clean pan, return to the boil and add Asian greens. Season with fish sauce and sesame oil. Taste to see if soup needs a little more fish sauce or perhaps a pinch of sugar. Add noodles and simmer 1–2 mins or until warm.

Ladle into large shallow bowls and place roasted duck on top. Sprinkle with green onons (shallots) and coriander leaves. Serve immediately.

Wine:
These are somewhat unusual flavours, but like most soups will be well complemented by a sherry.

Beef and Udon Noodle Soup

Asian soups like Vitenamese pho have become a popular lunchtime take-away for office workers but they are easy to make at home.

Serves: 4
Preparation time: 5–10 mins
Cooking time: 15 mins

1 tablespoon peanut oil
600 g (1⅓ lb) rump steak
½ bunch green onions (shallots)
2 carrots, peeled and sliced
150 g (5 oz) mushrooms, sliced
5cm (2in) piece fresh ginger, grated
2 cloves garlic, crushed
1–2 red chillies, deseeded and chopped (optional)
1 litre (2 pints) beef consommé or beef stock
350 g (11½ oz) packet fresh udon noodles

Heat 1 tablespoon of oil over high heat in a large saucepan. Brown beef on both sides. Remove and rest. Add remaining ingredients, except noodles to pan, bring to the boil and simmer until carrot is soft, around 10 minutes. Taste and if desired, dilute with a little boiling water.

Thinly slice beef across the grain. Add beef and noodles to the soup. Return just to the boil and serve immediately.

Wine:
A sherry is always wonderful with a soup, especially one with Asian flavours.

Fennel and Mushroom Salad

The ultimate fast and easy recipe with no cooking at all, yet with the most marvellous flavours relying on good quality produce. Use either baby fennel or a larger bulb, having first discarded the tough outer leaves. The mushrooms should also be very fresh.

Serves: 4
Preparation time: 10 mins
Cooking time: Nil

1 bulb fennel
100 g (3½ oz) button mushrooms
2 tablespoons extra virgin olive oil
50 g (1¾ oz) parmesan cheese
rock salt and freshly ground black pepper

Finely slice the fennel and mushrooms. (Japanese slicers are good for this.) Arrange in individual serving bowls. Sprinkle with extra virgin olive oil, shavings of fresh parmesan, rock salt and freshly ground black pepper.

Wine:
These delicate flavours need a subtle white wine like a chenin blanc, marsanne or roussanne.

I love cooking with what is at hand. Here I cook from an unseen box with John Newton for a dinner at a Gastronomy Symposium.

Roasted Tomato and Spring Onion Salad

This is a fast and easy version of a restaurant quality dish. I use ripe, red, vine-ripened tomatoes for the best flavour in this dish.

Serves: 4
Preparation time: 5 mins
Cooking time: Up to 60 mins

extra virgin olive oil
6–8 ripe red tomatoes, skin on, cut in half
1 bunch spring onions
½ teaspoon sugar
½ teaspoon salt
½ bunch rocket (arugula), shredded

Preheat the oven to 125–150°C (250–300°F, Gas Mark 9).

Slosh some extra virgin olive oil in a baking dish. In it place the tomatoes, cut side uppermost, and a bunch of spring onions either left whole or cut carefully in half so they will still hold together. Sprinkle with the sugar and salt. Drizzle with more olive oil. Place in the oven for up to one hour or until the tomatoes are nicely softened and the shallots beginning to brown.

Divide between serving plates. Top with the rocket and a good drizzle of the pan juices. Serve hot, tepid or cold.

Wine:
An aged semillon or riesling match the sweet, developed tomato flavours.

Real Spanish Gazpacho

This recipe comes from Andalusia in Spain. Traditionally it would be made by pounding the ingredients together with a wooden pestle. This technique is at the basis of Spanish food. However, it works well using a food processor. An ideal chilled soup for the steamy summer months.

Serves: 4–6
Preparation time: 15 minutes
Cooking time: Nil

1 kg (2 lb) ripe summer tomatoes
50 g (1¾ oz) fresh white bread, crusts removed
2 garlic cloves, peeled and chopped
1 large red or green capsicum, chopped
1 small cucumber, peeled, deseeded and chopped
50 ml (1¾ fl oz) extra virgin olive oil
½ teaspoon sherry vinegar or wine vinegar to taste
coarse sea salt
freshly ground black pepper

Garnish (optional)
small pieces of bread
chopped green peppers
chopped cucumber

First peel and de-seed the tomatoes: make a small cross by cutting with a knife at the top of the tomatoes. Plunge into boiling water for a minute or two. Peel the skin off. Cut in half and give them a squeeze to remove the seeds. Set aside.

Make bread into breadcrumbs in the food processor. Remove. Chop garlic in processor and then add tomatoes, capsicum and cucumber and blend. Add the breadcrumbs and blend again. Gradually stir in the oil a drop at a time, the vinegar to taste, salt and a pinch of freshly ground pepper.

Dilute with a little water and blend again. Sieve (if you like) and place in the fridge. Serve cold.

Present the garnish in small dishes and place in the centre of the table for people to serve themselves.

Cook's note:
You can make this all even quicker by processing the whole tomatoes with everything else and sieving before adding the breadcrumbs. These also make a great finger food item, served in shot glasses!

Wine:
Well, it's Spanish so a sherry of course!

Bridge Climb with my daughter Lucy.

With my co-host of Fresh on the Nine Network, Peter Evans.

My friend Tetsuya Wakuda of world-famous Tetsuya's Restaurant launched my food and wine matching book Balance, co-authored by Colin Corney.

LARGE PLATES

Deep-fried Bean Curd with Chilli Sauce

Some time ago I visited Club Med at Cherating, Malaysia. At Kuala Lumpur Airport I was met by friends who took me to a restaurant literally at the end of the runway. This dish so impressed me that I was determined to recreate it. For simplicity, I use a commercial chilli sauce as the base.

Serves: 4
Preparation time: 10 mins
Cooking time: 10 mins + 10 mins marinating

625 g (1¼ lb) firm tofu or bean curd
¼ cup (2 fl oz) salt-reduced soy sauce
or kecap manis (Indonesian soy sauce)
oil, for deep frying e.g. peanut, grapeseed

Chilli Sauce
1 tablespoon peanut oil
2 cloves garlic, chopped
2 eschalots, chopped
¾ cup (6 fl oz) chilli sauce
1 tablespoons Thai fish sauce
1 teaspoon sugar
5 tablespoons (3 fl oz) water

To serve
½ bunch green onions (shallots), sliced
2 red chillies, sliced, for garnish

Drain tofu, slice and marinate in soy sauce for at least 10 minutes.

To make chilli sauce, heat oil and fry garlic and eschalots until softening. Add chilli sauce, fish sauce, sugar and water and simmer for 1–2 minutes. Taste. If it is too hot, thin with more water.

Heat oil in a saucepan or deep-fryer. Drain bean curd and pat dry on paper towels. Deep-fry bean curd briefly, in batches in hot oil. Drain and place on serving dish. Top with sauce and green onions.

The inside of the bean curd will be wondrously silky and soft, demonstrating why texture is such an important consideration in Asian food.

Wine:
This is a fiery dish, so choose a gewürztraminer, riesling, sauvignon blanc or pinot noir.

Gnocchi with Pumpkin, Horseradish and Spinach

This is an unusual combination that makes a delicious pasta sauce. You can just throw it together, relying on your tastebuds rather than use specific quantities.

Serves: Approx 8, depending on the size of the pumpkin
Preparation time: 10 mins
Cooking time: 65 mins

1 butternut pumpkin, approx. 1.5 kg (3 lb)
2 tablespoons honey
3 red chillies, seeded and chopped
1 teaspoon horseradish
1¼ cups (10 fl oz) fresh cream
1 cup (8 fl oz) chicken stock
salt and pepper
nutmeg
1 kg (2 lb) gnocchi
½ bunch spinach or 1 bunch silverbeet

Pre-heat oven to 200°C (400°F, Gas Mark 6).

Peel the butternut pumpkin and cut into chunks. Place in a baking dish and drizzle with honey and roast until soft, around an hour. Purée the pumpkin in a food processor, then place in a saucepan over medium heat. Add the chillies, a teaspoon or more of horseradish, fresh cream, a cup or so of chicken stock (more if the pumpkin is large), salt, pepper and nutmeg to taste. Bring to a simmer. (This can also be done in the microwave). Meanwhile cook gnocchi according to packet instructions.

Roll up some leaves of spinach into a cigar shape and slice finely to make a chiffonnade. Stir through the sauce and serve over hot pasta.

Cook's note:
It's important to match you pasta to the sauce you are using. Thick sauces like this one need a chunky pasta which can stand up to it—it could even be pasta shells or rigatoni.

Wine:
The full, rounded flavours of a rich chardonnay stand up to both the texture and flavour of the sauce, the tannins in the wine cleansing the mouth between mouthfuls.

Glass Noodle Salad

I love the light, transparent look of cellophane noodles. This salad doesn't take long to make and can be assembled, except for the peanuts, several hours ahead. It's very cooling in hot weather and can be given more substance by adding shredded chicken, pork or prawns at the last minute.

Serves: 4–6
Preparation time: 10 mins
Cooking time: 10 mins soaking

125 g (4 oz) mung or green bean vermicelli (cellophane noodles)
2 tablespoons lime or lemon juice
1 tablespoon Thai fish sauce (nam pla)
2 tablespoons Thai sweet chilli sauce
1 large red onion, sliced
3 tablespoons green onions (shallots), chopped
2 tablespoons fresh coriander (cilantro), finely chopped
2 tablespoons fresh mint leaves, finely chopped
90 g (3 oz) peanuts (good quality, shelled and lightly salted)

Soak cellophane noodles in warm water for 10 minutes. Drain. Combine lime juice, fish sauce and chilli sauce (an easy way is to shake well in a screw-top jar). Pour over drained noodles and toss to mix through.

Add onion, green onions, coriander and mint and toss through gently. Just before serving, toss peanuts through.

Wine:
Choose a fragrant gewürztraminer to accompany this aromatic, spicy dish.

Laksa

Shrimp paste and sambal oelek are available from Asian food stores, as are fresh Laksa noodles. However, if you prefer, any dried rice noodle such as rice vermicelli can be used or you can use a combination.

Serves: 4–6
Preparation time: 10 mins
Cooking time: 15 mins

200 g (7 oz) approx. dried rice noodles
300 g (10 oz)fresh Laksa noodles
1 tablespoon peanut oil or light olive oil with a dash of sesame oil
4 eshallots, chopped
1 stalk lemon grass, finely sliced
1 teaspoon shrimp paste
2 teaspoons sambal oelek or chilli purée
1 tablespoon good quality curry powder
1 cup (8 fl oz) fish stock
3 cups (1½ pints) coconut milk
300 g (10 oz) green prawns, shelled and deveined
300 g (10 oz) firm white fish, for example, silver warehou
juice of 1 lime
salt and pepper
1 bunch mint
1–2 cups bean sprouts
1 cucumber, grated

Put the dried noodles into boiling water for several minutes (the microwave speeds up this process). Add the fresh noodles when the dried ones are soft.

Stir fry the eshallots, lemon grass, shrimp paste and sambal oelek or chilli purée in the oils for a minute or two, until they are aromatic. Add the curry powder and cook for a minute before adding the fish stock. Bring to the boil and simmer for 5–10 minutes to fully develop the flavours. Add the coconut milk, heat until just boiling, then add prawns and fish.

The seafood will cook quickly, taking only a few minutes. When it is cooked, remove from the heat, add the lime juice and season to taste with salt and pepper. Drain the noodles. Place a handful in each bowl then top with the hot laksa. Serve with a side garnish of mint leaves, bean sprouts and grated cucumber.

Wine:
Spice and coconut milk can both be handled by a shiraz which has been matured in American oak, or a pinot noir.

Pasta with Prawns and Chilli Oil

Chilli oil is fiery, so use it with care and to suit your own taste.

Serves: 4
Preparation time: 10 mins
Cooking time: 10 mins

500 g (1 lb) tagliolini or linguine
olive oil
500 g (1 lb) medium-sized green prawns,
peeled and deveined
1 bunch English spinach
chilli oil
1–2 ripe red tomatoes, finely diced

Cook the pasta in plenty of salted, boiling water until al dente—tender, but firm to the bite.

While it is cooking, heat some olive oil in a pan and quickly cook the prawns. This takes only a couple of minutes. When almost cooked, add some leaves of English spinach and cook until wilted.

Drain the pasta, toss it in the pan with the prawns and spinach add a drizzle of chilli oil (and some more olive oil if you like) and the diced tomatoes.

Wine:
Pinot noir can suit the intensity of this recipe or try a rosé with a little residual sugar.

Cataplana

Shellfish and pork is a popular combination in Portugal. Legend has it that it was used during the Inquisition as a double whammy to test religious zeal as pork and shellfish are forbidden to Jews and Moslems.

Serves: 6
Preparation time: 10 mins + 30 mins soaking
Cooking time: 15 mins

1 kg (2 lb) clams or vongole
¼ cup salt, approx.
¼ cup (1 oz) cornmeal (polenta), approx.
olive oil
1 medium red onion, chopped
1 medium onion, chopped
1 red capsicum
3 cloves garlic, chopped
1 bay leaf
4 large red, ripe tomatoes, peeled, seeded and chopped
1 tablespoon tomato paste
½ cup (4 fl oz) white wine
155 g (5 oz) piece prosciutto (presunto is the Portuguese style) or smoked ham
1 chourico (the Portuguese version), chorizo or pepperoni, coarsely chopped
2 tablespoons Continental parsley, chopped
freshly ground black pepper

To clean clams, soak in plenty of cold water with salt and cornmeal added for at least 30 minutes. This purges the clams of grit. Rinse, wash, and rinse again.

Heat oil and cook onions over low heat until they begin to soften. Add capsicum and garlic and cook until all are softened, sweet and soft but not brown. Increase heat and add bay leaf, tomato, tomato paste and wine and bring to the boil. Reduce heat to medium and simmer until tomato is broken down and the sauce is pulpy. Stir in prosciutto or ham and chourico and cook for 5 minutes more.

Add clams to pot, mix through the sauce and cover with a tight-fitting lid. Cook for only 3–5 minutes, or until clams open. (Discard any that do not open.) Serve immediately, sprinkled with parsley and seasoned with black pepper to taste.

Cook's note:
A cataplana is a hinged metal container that can be clamped shut. A pan with a tight-fitting lid works fine.

Wine:
For this dish choose a rose or light style of red wine, such as pinot noir or chambourcin. For a different approach, try a chilled fino sherry.

Portuguese-style Clams

I have been lucky enough to visit Portugal and enjoy the country's unique cuisine which, naturally enough in a seafaring nation, features lots of seafood. I found this delicious dish easy to reproduce here with clams, which are not used as often as they deserve to be.

Serves: 4
Preparation time: 5 mins + 30 mins soaking
Cooking time: 5 mins

1 kg (2 lb) clams or vongole
¼ cup salt, approx.
¼ cup cornmeal, approx.
1–2 tablespoons extra virgin olive oil
¼–½ cup (2–4 fl oz) white wine
2 cloves garlic, chopped
3 tablespoons flat-leaf parsley, freshly chopped

To serve
fresh bread
(such as the wonderful Portuguese broa)

To clean clams, soak in plenty of cold water with salt and cornmeal added for at least 30 minutes. This purges the clams of grit. Rinse, wash, and rinse again.

Heat olive oil in a frying-pan, add clams, wine, garlic and parsley. Cover and place over medium to high heat for a few minutes only—you will hear a cracking sound as the clams open. Once open, they are ready to eat. Serve immediately with fresh bread to sop up the juices.

Wine:
Choose any light style of white wine, or even a rose, with this dish.

Prawn Risotto with Saffron

Nearly every good cook treasures a version of this recipe. This is my special one—I hope you like it.

Serves: 6 as an entree, 4 as a main course
Preparation time: 10 mins
Cooking time: 30 mins

1 litre (2 pints) chicken or fish stock
1 teaspoon saffron threads
½ cup (4 fl oz) olive oil
1 onion, finely chopped
2 teaspoons garlic, crushed
2 chillies, seeded and finely chopped
345 g (11 oz) Arborio rice
¾ cup (6 fl oz) white wine
18 large or 24–30 smaller green prawns,
shelled and deveined
½ bunch basil, leaves only, cut into a
chiffonnade (see cook's note)
sea salt and freshly ground black pepper
60 g (2 oz) butter

Cook's note:

Make a stack of about 10 basil leaves, roll up tightly into a cigar shape and slice very finely across the roll. Repeat with remaining leaves. This is called a chiffonade.

Wine:

Choose a semillon or pinot noir as the ideal partner for this risotto.

Bring fish stock to the boil either in a saucepan or in the microwave. Infuse saffron threads in stock.

Heat oil in a heavy-based pan and cook onion, garlic and chilli until soft. Add rice and stir to coat with oil. Add wine, stir and cook until absorbed. Now begin to add simmering stock, about ½ cup (4 fl oz) at a time. It is imperative that the stock is at simmering point when it is added to the rice. Stir well after each addition and let the rice absorb the liquid before adding more.

When the rice is almost cooked and risotto is creamy, add prawns and basil. Keep stirring until prawns are cooked, about 3 minutes. Season to taste with salt and pepper. Stir in butter to finish and serve as soon as it has melted.

Microwave method:

(For half quantity—full quantity will require a little longer cooking.) All cooking done on HIGH.

Heat oil and onion in a large microwave-proof dish, uncovered, for 2 minutes, add garlic and chilli and cook for 1 minute more. Add rice, stir to coat with oil, and cook, uncovered for 1 minute. Add wine, stir and cook for 2 minutes more, or until absorbed. Add all the stock and the saffron to the dish. Cover and cook for 12 minutes.

Add prawns and basil and cook for 3 minutes more. Season to taste with salt and pepper. Stir in butter to finish and serve as soon as it has melted.

Seafood Paella

Serves 4–6

Preparation time: 10 mins

Cooking time: 30 mins + 35 mins for stock

Stock

⅓ cup (2¾ fl oz) extra virgin olive oil
2 cloves garlic
1 teaspoon hot or sweet smoked paprika
2 ripe tomatoes
prawn heads and shells from 500 g (1 lb)
green prawns (see below)
1.75 litres (3½ pints) fish or chicken stock

Paella

100 ml (3½ fl oz) extra virgin olive oil
2 cloves garlic
1 teaspoon hot or sweet smoked paprika
2 ripe tomatoes, roughly chopped
500 g (1 lb) calasparra, or shortgrain, rice
1.5 litre (3 pints) hot stock (see above)
pinch saffron threads (optional)
salt flakes, to taste
250 g (8 oz) calamari or cuttlefish, cleaned
and sliced
500 g (1 lb) green prawns, shelled
chopped flat-leaf parsley

Cook's note:

If using a pan with even heat distribution,
all cooking can be done on the cooktop.
Otherwise, when the rice rises (after about 15
minutes), top with seafood and put the pan in a
180°C (350°F, Gas Mark 4) oven for 4 minutes.

Stock

First make the seafood stock by heating oil in a large saucepan and cook garlic, paprika and tomato over medium heat. After a few minutes, add prawn shells and heads and when brown, cover with stock. Bring to the boil and simmer for at least 30 minutes. Strain, discarding solids.

Paella

Heat the olive oil in a paella pan or heavy-based frying pan and fry garlic, paprika and tomatoes, stirring frequently until brown and tomatoes are broken down (this is called picada or sofrito and is used in most paellas in Spain).

Add the rice. Mix well and let the rice brown for a couple of minutes.

Add the hot seafood stock (above), saffron and salt and mix all the ingredients together. DO NOT STIR AGAIN.

Bring to the boil over high heat then reduce heat to a slow simmer and cook for a further 15 minutes or until rice is almost tender.

Place the calamari and prawns on top. Cover the pan with a large piece of foil and simmer, covered, for about five minutes or until prawns are opaque. Remove from the heat, add parsley and leave to rest, loosely covered with foil for at least 3 minutes before serving.

Wine:

Choose a Spanish wine to accompany this Iberian classic, or a semillon, pinot noir or chambourcin.

Marinated Baby Octopus

Many nations have a version of this dish. In Portugal, it would customarily be served at the beginning of the meal as one of a number of dishes placed on the table.

Serves: 6
Preparation time: 15 mins
Cooking time: 5 mins

750 g (1½ lb) baby octopus
½ cup (4 fl oz) red wine vinegar
½ onion, sliced
1 bay leaf
½ teaspoon whole black peppercorns
½ large red onion, finely chopped
2 red chillies, finely chopped
2 cloves garlic, finely chopped
¼ cup (2 fl oz) lemon juice (1 small lemon)
1 cup (8 fl oz) extra virgin olive oil
1 cup freshly chopped herbs, e.g. parsley, coriander (cilantro)
2 tablespoons freshly chopped mint

If the octopus are not already prepared, cut off their heads and remove and discard the small hard 'beak' that remains in the top.

Cover remaining tentacles with vinegar, onion, bay leaf and peppercorns and add cold water to cover, about 2 cups (16 fl oz), depending on the size of the saucepan. Bring to the boil and drain immediately. Combine red onion, chilli, garlic, lemon juice, olive oil and herbs and season to taste. Refrigerate until ready to serve. Serve with octopus and crusty bread.

Cook's note:
Tenderise octopus by placing in a bowl, cover with boiling water, allow to stand for 1–2 minutes, drain, refresh under cold water. Repeat to a total of three times. This makes it easy to peel the main part of the octopus but not the tentacles if you wish.

Wine:
Choose a rosé or light style of red wine.

Modern Salad Niçoise

If you never liked traditional Salad Niçoise with tinned tuna, try this with fabulous fresh ingredients and you will soon change your mind.

Serves: 4
Preparation time: 10 mins
Cooking time: 20–30 mins

500 g (1 lb) fresh tuna
olive oil
mixed lettuce
500 g (1 lb) baby new potatoes, boiled, peeled and sliced
250 g (8 oz) cherry tomatoes
½ cup black olives
3 hardboiled eggs, sliced
1 small tin of anchovies (optional)
350 g (12½ oz) beans, blanched and sliced

Dressing
6 tablespoons olive oil
2 tablespoons wine vinegar
salt and pepper
1 teaspoon French mustard
2 tablespoons chopped fresh herbs (parsley, tarragon, basil)

Place tuna in a dish that fits it snugly. Cover with olive oil and cook in the oven at 150°C (300°F, Gas Mark 2) for 20–30 minutes, until just done. Cool in the oil. Remove from the oil, drain and slice into chunks.

Layer lettuce, potatoes, cherry tomatoes, olives, eggs, anchovies, beans and tuna in a dish.

Combine the dressing ingredients in a jar and shake vigorously. Pour over the salad and serve.

Cook's note:
To save time you could sear the tuna in a hot pan, browning all over

Wine:
Try one of the more delicate white wines like roussanne or marsanne, or even a rosé.

Tuna with Anchovy Sauce

This is another recipe developed for a Seafood Soirée. Here I was thrown the challenge of developing a fish recipe to go with cabernet.

Serves: 6
Preparation time: 10 mins
Cooking time: 15 mins

6 tuna steaks
3 cloves garlic
2 tablespoons parsley
2 tablespoons coriander
2 tablespoons basil
olive oil
small black olives, such as Ligurian

Sauce
375 ml (12½ fl oz) fish or beef stock
200 ml (7 fl oz) red wine
6 good quality anchovies, washed
2 tablespoons thick cream, or more to taste

Wine:
Whatever red wine you used in the sauce will go well, but my pick is a cabernet sauvignon.

Preheat the oven to 200°C (400°F, Gas Mark 6). Have some oven trays in oven to heat.

Bring the fish stock and wine to the boil in a saucepan and simmer to reduce. Trim any dark flesh from the tuna.

With the food processor motor running, chop the garlic and herbs. Alternatively, you can do this by hand. Dip the edges only of the tuna steaks in this mixture.

When the fish stock and wine has reduced to 200 ml (7 fl oz) or less, remove from heat and cool slightly. Blend with the anchovies. Return to the heat and stir in a good dollop of thick cream. Beware, however, of the salt content of this dish. Taste the sauce, it is unlikely that it will need any additional salt. It may instead need extra cream.

Heat the olive oil in a pan and, when hot, seal the tuna steaks on one side until brown and crisp—only a minute or two. Place the uncooked side down on hot oven trays and cook in the hot oven for 5 minutes and no more. If you have oven trays which can go on the hot plate everything can be done on the tray from the initial browning to the baking. (Alternatively just cook the tuna in the pan. Using the oven allows more to be cooked at once.)

Plate the tuna, pour over the sauce, scatter with olives and serve with garlic mash (unsalted if the sauce is salty) or whole baby potatoes tossed in olive oil and crisp green beans or salad.

Tuna with Wasabi and Fresh Herb Butter

Fish frightens many home cooks, but cooked simply and quickly it is delicious, stylish and, above all, fast and easy. The quality of tuna in our markets is always superb, as it must be to be suitable for eating raw as sashimi. This dish turns tuna sashimi with soy sauce and wasabi on its head for a delightful and different result.

Serves: 4
Preparation time: 10 mins
Cooking time: 6 mins

olive oil
4 thick tuna steaks
grape tomatoes, to serve
salad mix
balsamic vinegar
olive oil

Wasabi and Herb Butter

1 clove garlic
1 tablespoon chopped fresh coriander (cilantro)
2 tablespoons other chopped fresh herbs of your choice, such as dill or chives
2 tablespoons prepared wasabi paste or powder
2 teaspoons Dijon mustard
2 teaspoons soy sauce
freshly ground black pepper
250 g (8 oz) butter, softened

To make the wasabi and herb butter, mince the garlic in a food processor with the herbs. Then add the wasabi, mustard, soy sauce, pepper and butter and blend. Turn out on a piece of greaseproof paper, foil or plastic wrap and form into a fat sausage. Freeze or refrigerate to harden until it is required.

Heat a pan with a little olive oil. When it is very hot, put the tuna steaks in it, brown them on one side and then turn them over. The aim is to have the fish brown and crisp on the outside and pink on the inside. Serve immediately topped with a slice of the wasabi butter, grape tomatoes and some salad mix from your greengrocer, over which a little balsamic vinegar and good olive oil has been drizzled.

You will find that this recipe makes more than enough butter for four tuna steaks, so I suggest that you freeze about half of the butter—it will be great for an impromptu meal.

Wine:

Wasabi can give a hit of heat yet the tuna is almost meaty so choose a pinot noir or unwooded chardonnay.

Grilled Bream with Cumin

This recipe is based on that in Diane Seed's Mediterranean Dishes. It is a simple and delicious way of cooking fish. If you don't like whole fish, use fillets instead, but be careful not to overcook them.

Serves: 4
Preparation time: 10 mins
Cooking time: 10 mins

5 tablespoons olive oil
3 teaspoons cumin
4 cloves garlic, minced
salt to taste
1 teaspoon harissa paste or sambal oelek
4 small bream or snapper, approximately 250 g (8 oz) each
4 desirée potatoes, washed
2 bunched baby bok choy, to serve

Mix together the oil, cumin, garlic, salt and harissa paste or sambal oelek. Trim fins and tail of fish with kitchen scissors. Make 2 or 3 deep diagonal cuts with a knife in each side of the fish, then put the fish in the marinade, pushing the marinade into the slashes.

Slice the unpeeled potatoes into rounds. Microwave them, covered, on HIGH for around 4 minutes or steam over boiling water on the cooktop.

Meanwhile preheat the grill. Cook the fish under the grill for 3–4 minutes each side. Place the potato rounds in with the fish, turning them once so that they are moistened by the marinade. They will be done at the same time as the fish. Serve with steamed baby bok choy.

Wine:
Although this is fish, there is a fair bit of flavour and spice going on here so try a pinot noir.

Quick Fish Curry

Curries are easy to cook. Once you've mastered the technique you can adapt the recipe by adding spices of your choice or replacing the fish with meat. I love fish because it is quick, ideal for television demonstration. Of course, meat would require longer cooking.

Serves: 4
Preparation time: 10 mins
Cooking time: 10 mins

½ tablespoon vegetable oil
2 teaspoons finely chopped or grated ginger
2 cloves garlic, finely chopped
1 small onion, finely chopped
1 teaspoon cumin seeds (optional)
1 teaspoon ground cumin (optional)
1 tablespoon curry paste
1½ cups (12 fl oz) coconut cream
salt and freshly ground black pepper
600 g (1⅓ lb) firm white fish fillets, cut into large chunks
½ teaspoon chilli paste (optional)
2 tablespoon chopped coriander (cilantro) leaves
cooked jasmine rice, to serve

Heat the oil and fry the ginger, garlic and onion for a few minutes to develop their distinctive flavours. Add the cumin seeds and cumin, if you are using them. Now add the curry paste. Stir well and pour in the coconut cream. Bring to a simmer and season with salt and pepper. Add the fish and poach for 3–4 minutes without boiling. The fish should be opaque.

Serve with jasmine rice and garnish with coriander leaves.

Alternatively, taste the curry and, if you prefer a spicier curry, combine the coriander leaves with the chilli paste and stir through before serving.

Variations:

- For a Thai-style curry, use Thai green or red curry paste, leave out the cumin and add a splash of Thai fish sauce.
- This recipe can easily be adapted for meat. Simply add the diced meat (chicken, beef, lamb or pork) after the curry paste. Cook for several minutes, stirring all the time to brown, and then add the coconut milk and proceed as before.

Wine:
Sauvignon blanc or pinot noir can handle the heat here without overwhelming the fish.

Grilled Thai Chicken

Thai is one of the most popular food styles, yet easy to enjoy at home. This recipe makes a terrific family meal.

Serves: 4
Preparation time: 10 mins + marinating
Cooking time: 12 mins

3 large garlic cloves
2–3cm (1–1½in) piece fresh ginger
1 large green chilli
2 small red chillies
1 bunch coriander (cilantro)
2 tablespoons caster sugar
grated zest and juice of 2 limes or 1 lemon
2 tablespoons kecap manis
(Indonesian soy sauce)
4 chicken breast fillets or 8 chicken thigh fillets
4 tablespoons cashews
rice sticks or rice noodles

With the motor of your food processor running, add the garlic, ginger, green chilli, red chillies, coriander and sugar in succession and process until well blended. Then add grated zest and juice of limes or lemon and kecap manis. Cut diagonal slashes in chicken fillets and pour over the marinade. Leave for an hour or so if possible, although this is not crucial.

Toast cashews, either in the microwave, oven or by frying. Soften the rice sticks or noodles in boiling water. Remove the chicken from the marinade. Grill or barbecue until done, about 6 minutes on each side.

Boil the remaining marinade for at least one minute. Drain the rice sticks or noodles, toss through most of marinade. Serve the noodles with the chicken on top and a little marinade poured over, finished with cashews and accompanied by a green salad.

Wine:
This dish is aromatic and spicy, so try a riesling, verdelho or sauvignon blanc.

Spring Salmon

Serves: 2
Preparation time: 10 mins
Cooking time: 20 mins

2 x 160–180 g (5–6 oz) skinless fillets of salmon or trout
white pepper
1 clove garlic, finely sliced
1¼ cups (10 fl oz) virgin olive oil, more or less
1 red capsicum, seeded and cut into strips
1 extra clove garlic, very finely sliced
2 fresh mushrooms, sliced
¼ bunch green onions (shallots), sliced
2 tablespoons rice vinegar
½ tablespoon kecap manis (Indonesian soy sauce)
sea salt to taste (optional)
baby salad leaves, to serve

Preheat the oven to the lowest setting, usually around 50°–90°C (120–190°F, Gas Mark 1).

Season salmon with pepper. Place in an ovenproof dish that just fits the two fish fillets. Sprinkle with slivers of garlic and cover completely with olive oil. Place in the oven for no more than 15 minutes, until the fish is just done and still pink inside. Remove the salmon fillets from the oil and drain on a paper towel.

Using a little of the oil from the fish, sauté the capsicum, additional garlic, mushrooms and green onions until the capsicum is soft but not brown. Add the rice vinegar and kecap manis to the pan. Shake.

Place a piece of salmon on each plate, sprinkle with sea salt to taste and pour over contents of pan. Serve warm or at room temperature. It is best not to refrigerate this dish as this may harden the fish. Accompany with a salad of small leaves such as mizuna, baby endive, etc.

Wine:

The luscious texture of this dish demands the equally-luscious mouthfeel from an elegant, wooded chardonnay, though red wine drinkers would be happy with a pinot noir.

Alternative method:

To decrease the absorption of oil by the fish, brush the salmon with extra-virgin olive oil, sprinkle with pepper and wrap tightly in foil. Cook in the oven in the same way and proceed as for the previous method.

Cook's note:

This salmon is also delicious sliced like sashimi and served with soy sauce.

Whole Baby Snapper with Tomato and Lime Salsa

Whole fish is quite a different proposition from fillets. It is more economical, easier to present well and retains moisture and flavour beautifully—as long as you and your guests can cope with the bones.

Serves: 6
Preparation time: 15 mins
Cooking time: 10–12 mins

6 whole baby snapper (1 per person), scaled and cleaned
juice of 1 lemon
½ cup (4 fl oz) dry white wine
coriander (cilantro) leaves, for garnish

Tomato and lime salsa

1 large or 2 small tomatoes, about 125 g (4 oz), seeded and diced
½ green capsicum, about 60 g (2 oz), seeded and diced
½ red capsicum, about 60 g (2 oz), seeded and diced
½ medium red onion, chopped
½ bunch coriander (cilantro), chopped
juice and rind of 1 lime
few drops Tabasco sauce
1 tablespoon balsamic vinegar
¼ cup (2 fl oz) olive oil
salt and freshly ground pepper

Preheat oven to moderate, 180°–190°C (350°–375°F, Gas Mark 4). Trim fins of fish. Slash each through to the bone on one side, place in a baking dish and sprinkle with lemon juice and/or white wine. Cover with foil and bake for 10–12 minutes (when fish is cooked it will be opaque and flake easily away from the bones). Alternatively, if you are a little daunted by whole fish, pan-fry or steam snapper or bream fillets.

Meanwhile, combine salsa ingredients.

To serve, spoon salsa over fish, especially where it has been slashed so that the flavours can be absorbed. Garnish with coriander leaves.

Wine:
Choose a riesling or semillon for this fresh-flavoured dish with only a hint of heat.

Fish with Chermoula Marinade and Couscous

Chermoula is a traditional Moroccan marinade or sauce. Each family has its own, usually secret, recipe. Couscous is the perfect accompaniment to this fish dish, and it would also complement many other recipes in this book.

Serves: 6
Preparation time: 5 mins + resting
Cooking time: 5–8 mins

6 pieces firm fish such as ling
lemon wedges

Marinade
juice and grated rind of 1 lemon
1 teaspoon ground cumin
1 teaspoon ground coriander (cilantro)
2 teaspoons sweet paprika
3 tablespoons olive oil
2 tablespoons chopped parsley
2 tablespoons chopped coriander
pinch of salt

Couscous
200 g (7 oz) instant couscous
1 cup (8 fl oz) stock
2 tablespoons mixed dried fruits
2 red chillies
2 tablespoons toasted pine nuts
2 tablespoons chopped coriander (cilantro)
salt
pepper

Combine the marinade ingredients in a food processor. Place the fish in a shallow dish and pour marinade over it. Cover and, if possible, let the fish marinate for up to 20 minutes in the fridge. Place the fish under a pre-heated grill, basting it with the extra marinade while grilling. Fish is cooked when opaque. If there is any remaining marinade, boil for at least a minute and serve as a sauce with the fish and lemon wedges.

To prepare the couscous, pour the stock or water over the couscous and leave it to swell.

Pour a little boiling water over the dried fruit to plump them up. Seed and finely chop the chillies. Combine the couscous, chillies, dried fruit, pine nuts, coriander, salt and pepper. Heat in a pan with a little olive oil, stirring frequently, or in the microwave.

Cook's note:
Chermoula also makes a great marinade for lamb cutlets.

Wine:
This is well suited to many white wines from verdelho and unwooded chardonnay to viognier and pinot gris.

Whole Thai-style Steamed Fish with Chilli, Garlic and Coriander

Using a Chinese bamboo steamer is a wonderful way to cook fish. Scoring the flesh makes it easy to cook evenly and see when it is cooked. The sauce also makes a great accompaniment.

Serves: 2
Preparation time: 10 mins
Cooking time: 10 mins

3 large fresh chillies (red and/or green)
1 bunch fresh coriander (cilantro)
2 cloves garlic
1 tablespoon finely chopped ginger
2 x plate-size fish, eg. snapper or bream, or 1 large fish
1 tablespoon vegetable oil
1½ tablespoons sugar
1½ tablespoons Thai fish sauce
½ cup (4 fl oz) chicken or fish stock, or water
1 tablespoon lime or lemon juice
2 fresh red chillies or red capsicum, cut into fine julienne strips
whole sprigs of coriander (cilantro)
cooked jasmine rice, to serve

Wine:
The hot and spicy flavours here demand a wine which can soothe such as a sauvignon blanc, gewürztraminer or pinot noir.

Put the chillies, one coriander root from the bunch, garlic and ginger together in a food processor and blend, or pound together to make a paste.

Trim the fish tails and fins with scissors, wash and pat the fish dry. Score the flesh in three parallel lines on both sides. Place in a greased, Chinese bamboo steamer over boiling water. Alternatively, you can place the fish on greased foil and grill, sprinkle with a little lemon juice and white wine and bake in the oven or even fry it.

Heat the oil in a saucepan over a medium to high heat and fry the spice paste, sugar and fish sauce, stirring frequently, until the sugar dissolves and the mixture bubbles. Pour in the stock, stir, bring to the boil and simmer for a few minutes. Stir in the lime or lemon juice. Taste. If necessary add more sugar, fish sauce or lemon or lime juice remembering the classic Thai balance between hot, sour, sweet and salty.

Place the fish on individual serving plates and pour the sauce over the top. Sprinkle with chopped coriander leaves, julienne of chilli or capsicum and coriander sprigs. Serve with jasmine rice.

Fish with Rocket and Anchovy Butter

I love this butter for its simple way of jazzing up a piece of plain white fish and for the wonderful bright green the butter goes as it melts on the fish.

Serves: 6
Preparation time: 5 mins
Cooking time: 6 mins

1 tablespoon butter
1 tablespoon olive oil
6 large skinless fish fillets
(e.g. snapper, gemfish or ling)
rocket leaves (arugula), to serve

Rocket and Anchovy Butter
8 large leaves rocket
5 anchovy fillets
100 g (3½ oz) butter

To prepare rocket and anchovy butter, chop rocket and anchovies in a food processor. Add butter and process until smooth. Place on plastic wrap or foil and roll up into a thick sausage shape. Chill until required.

To cook fish, melt butter with oil in a large frying pan over high heat. Pan-fry fish fillets for only about 3 minutes each side, until cooked through and opaque. Lift from the pan and flip over so that the side that was cooked second is uppermost on the plate. Place each piece of fish on a simple bed of rocket leaves, top with a slice or two of rocket and anchovy butter and serve immediately.

Cook's note:
If there's any rocket and anchovy butter left over, it will keep indefinitely in the freezer. Zap up chicken, potato or any type of fish simply by topping with a slice of this tangy butter.

Wine:
An unoaked or lightly oaked chardonnay will balance the butter in this dish, without its taste becoming bitter because of the rocket.

Chicken Breasts with Red Capsicum Aïoli

Chicken breasts need good, strong flavours to make them interesting. Red capsicum, especially roasted, makes anything taste good! Made into an aïoli it is particularly delicious.

Serves: 6
Preparation time: 5 mins
Cooking time: 10 mins

Red Capsicum Aïoli
1 red capsicum
4 cloves garlic
1–2 egg yolks
salt
1–2 tablespoons lemon juice
2/3 cup (5 fl oz) olive oil

Chicken Breasts
6 chicken breasts
olive oil
12 slices of prosciutto (not too wafer thin)
mixed salad greens
1 punnet cherry tomatoes, halved

Wine:
Capsicum has a special affinity with cabernet sauvignon but should you prefer a white wine a chardonnay can work in the same way, the drying tannins in the wine working well to cleanse the palate between mouthfuls.

Roast or char-grill the red capsicum until black and blistered. Place in a plastic bag while still hot and leave to cool. Peel and remove the seeds.

Make the aïoli by placing the garlic, egg yolks and salt in a blender or food processor and processing to a paste. Add the capsicum and lemon juice and purée. Gradually add the olive oil with the motor running. The slower the olive oil is poured in, the thicker the aïoli will be (it is really a mayonnaise). Taste and adjust seasoning with additional lemon juice, salt and pepper, if required.

Brush the chicken breasts with olive oil and place in a hot cast iron pan with grill markings (or on the barbecue). After 5 minutes or so, turn the chicken breasts over. There should be strong markings on it from the pan. Continue to cook on the other side. When almost done, add the prosciutto to the grill pan or barbecue.

To serve, place a bed of salad greens on each serving plate. Scatter halved cherry tomatoes around the edges. Place a chicken breast in the middle of each plate. Drizzle with red capsicum aïoli and top with two slices of crisp prosciutto.

Chicken In a Pot
with Preserved Lemon

This is a recipe inspired by a trip to Morocco—but this is, once more, my version.

Serves: 4

Preparation time: 10 mins

Cooking time: 60 mins + 5 mins standing

4 pieces free range chicken Maryland,
1 teaspoon ground cumin
1 teaspoon ground coriander (cilantro)
1 teaspoon ground cinnamon
salt and freshly ground black pepper
2 tablespoons olive oil
1 large onion, sliced
1 whole bulb garlic, approx15 cloves, peeled
250 g (8 oz) button mushrooms
½ cup (4 fl oz) white wine
1 cup (8 fl oz) chicken stock
2 carrots, coarsely chopped
2 whole red chillies, cut in half but held together by the stem
1 knob fresh ginger, peeled and sliced
1 preserved lemon, skin only, cut into strips
1 cup (8 fl oz) hot chicken stock, extra
125 g (4 oz) couscous

Wine:

Choose a young, unwooded semillon for a miraculous match with the preserved lemon in this dish.

Preheat oven to moderate, 180°–190°C (350°–375°F, Gas Mark 4).

Rub chicken skin with combined cumin, coriander, cinnamon, salt and pepper and set aside.

Warm 1 tablespoon oil in a large flameproof casserole and cook onion and garlic until lightly coloured. Add remaining oil and mushrooms and toss to coat with oil. Cook 2 minutes longer. Add wine and stock and bring to the boil. Add carrot, chillies, ginger and preserved lemon. Return to the boil. Plunge the chicken into this, turning it to tighten the skin. Seal casserole well with foil and a lid and bake, for 40 minutes. Alternatively, cook over very low heat on the cooktop.

Pour extra stock over couscous, cover with a clean cloth and leave to swell while the chicken is cooking. At the end of cooking time, remove chicken and add couscous to warm through in the wonderful broth and vegetables left in the pot. Replace chicken on top and stand, covered, for about 5 minutes.

To serve, ladle the aromatic broth with vegetables and couscous into 4 bowls and top each with a joint of chicken. Remove the chillies if you wish, but the long cooking will have transferred their flavour throughout the pot. The occasional bit of preserved lemon is a wonderful surprise.

Chicken in a Salt Crust

A classic recipe often used for beef, lamb or fish. The chicken steams inside the crust, remaining moist and flavoursome, but you must start with a good chicken.

Serves: 4
Preparation time: 15 mins
Cooking time: 100 mins + 15 mins resting

few sprigs of fresh rosemary
1 free-range or corn-fed chicken,
about 1.5 kg (3 lb)
2 tablespoons olive oil
freshly ground black pepper
1 tablespoon milk
roast potatoes, to serve
green beans, to serve

Salt Crust
1 kg (2 lb) plain flour
1 kg (2 lb) cooking salt
or coarse salt from the butcher
3¼ cups (1½ pints) cold water, approx.

Sauce
2 cups (16 fl oz) chicken stock
1½ cups (12 fl oz) dry white wine
2 tablespoons thick cream

Wine:
The flavour here is of pure, perfectly cooked chicken which is best matched with chardonnay.

Preheat oven to moderately hot, 200°–210°C (400°–425°F, Gas Mark 6). To make crust, combine flour and salt, pour in water and knead to a doughy consistency. You may need to add a little more water. (This quantity is too large and heavy for most food processors.)

On a lightly floured surface, roll out dough to an oval about 8mm (¼in) thick. Place half the rosemary in centre. Brush chicken with olive oil and season with pepper. Place chicken, breast-side-down, on dough. Brush outside edge of dough with milk. Place more herbs over chicken and fold dough over to encase it all. Seal all the joins carefully with milk. Turn dough bundle over and place, seam-side-down, on a baking tray. Bake for at least 1 hour. Remove from oven and leave to rest for 15 minutes. (Poussin or spatchcock can be done this way, too, but cooked for a shorter time.)

Meanwhile, to make sauce, heat combined stock and wine and boil vigorously to reduce. When reduced by half, stir in cream and keep warm.

Take chicken to the table in its crust. Cut around top of crust, remove and lift out chicken. Discard herbs and carve chicken. Serve with sauce, roast potatoes and green beans.

Mustard-crusted Chicken Breast with Fennel and Orange

I love mustard, crunchy food and fennel, but fennel is one of those vegetables that is often under-utilised. This recipe successfully combines my three loves.

Serves: 4
Preparation time: 10 mins
Cooking time: 18 mins

4 chicken breast fillets
crushed mustard seeds or mustard meal
30 g (1 oz) butter
1 tablespoon olive oil
⅔ cup (5 fl oz) chicken stock
1–2 tablespoons marmalade
2 bulbs fennel
2 tablespoons extra light olive oil
rind and juice of 2 oranges
½ bunch fresh mint, leaves only,
cut into a chiffonnade (see Cook's note)

Roll chicken fillets in crushed mustard seeds (if unavailable, crush whole seeds in a blender, pepper mill or with a mortar and pestle). Heat butter and oil in a heavy-based or non-stick pan and pan-fry chicken over high heat for 2 minutes each side to seal. Reduce heat to medium and continue to cook for about 10 minutes, or until cooked through. Remove from pan, increase heat and pour in chicken stock and marmalade. Boil vigorously for several minutes until mixture has a sauce-like consistency.

Meanwhile, prepare fennel by slicing bulbs very finely (a Japanese grater is ideal for the task). Pan-fry with oil and orange rind. Cook only briefly so that the fennel is still rather firm. Right at the end add the orange juice.

To serve, make a bed of fennel on each plate, slice each chicken breast in half and place on top. Throw mint into the sauce and spoon sauce onto chicken breast.

Wine:
Choose a zesty, fruity wine to best match the flavours of orange and mint, perhaps a riesling, semillon/sauvignon blanc or verdelho.

Cook's note:
Make a stack of about 10 mint leaves, roll up tightly into a cigar shape and slice very finely across the roll. Repeat with remaining leaves. This is called a chiffonnade.

Thai-Style Red Curry of Duck Livers

Thai curries have become firm favourites. Here, duck or chicken livers make a wonderful variation. If you don't like offal, substitute lamb or beef strips.

Serves: 6
Preparation time: 10 mins
Cooking time: 15 mins

1 kg (2 lb) duck or chicken livers
2 tablespoons peanut oil
3 cloves garlic, crushed
2.5cm (1in) piece fresh ginger, grated
2 tablespoons Thai red curry paste
3–4 red chillies (optional), seeded, finely chopped
2 cups (16 fl oz) coconut milk
3 kaffir lime leaves
1 tablespoon palm sugar (or brown sugar)
1 tablespoon Thai fish sauce (nam pla)
juice of 1 lime
¼ cup chopped fresh coriander (cilantro) leaves, for garnish
cooked jasmine rice, to serve
1 red chilli, extra, finely chopped for garnish (optional)

Trim duck or chicken livers. Heat oil in a wok or large saucepan over high heat and cook garlic, ginger, curry paste and chilli for 1 to 2 minutes, or until fragrant. Add livers and toss to coat in the curry paste. (If your pan is not large, it may be better to do this in batches, combining at the end.) Cook gently, turning frequently until livers are browned on the outside.

Add coconut milk, lime leaves, palm sugar and fish sauce. Reduce heat and simmer 5–10 minutes. Stir in lime juice. Taste and add more sugar, juice or fish sauce if required. Garnish with coriander leaves and serve with jasmine rice.

Cook's note:
if you can't get fresh kaffir lime leaves, use dried kaffir lime leaves, soaked in a little boiling water or substitute rind of 1 lime for the leaves.

Wine:
Choose a full-bodied shiraz to accompany a red curry. Cool-climate shiraz can have a peppery quality, similar to the spiciness of the curry, while warm-climate shiraz tends to be full and rich, complementing the curry like a chutney.

Pasta with Chicken Livers, Sage and Rocket

Chicken livers are one of those things you either love or hate. This is a great alternative to lambs fry and bacon.

Serves: 2
Preparation time: 5 mins
Cooking time: 12 mins

150 g (5 oz) pasta, such as ricciarelle
300 g (10 oz) chicken or duck livers extra-virgin olive oil
2 slices prosciutto or pancetta
handful of sage leaves
1 bunch rocket or arugula
salt and pepper

Cook the pasta in plenty of salted boiling water according to packet directions.

Trim livers. Get a frypan very hot and pour in some extra-virgin olive oil. Cook prosciutto until crisp. Drain on paper towel and reserve. Quickly sauté the livers. Add some sage leaves and cook for a few minutes only, so the livers are still pink inside.

Drain the pasta and place in serving bowls. Remove the frypan from the heat. Quickly throw into the pan some rocket, salt, freshly ground black pepper and a little extra olive oil (if there are not many pan juices) and stir lightly. Crumble in prosciutto. Pour over pasta and serve immediately.

Wine:

Sangiovese, the Italian grape variety of Chianti, is savoury and not too full-bodied, allowing the flavour of livers to shine through.

During the dreadful drought in Australia in 2004, Peter Howard and I cooked for the international performers in the 'green room' for the fundraising Farmhand Concert.

Spatchcock Dijonnaise

I am especially fond of Dijonnaise, a blend of Dijon, seeded mustard and mayonnaise, delicious on its own or a great shortcut to a sauce.

Serves: 6
Preparation time: 10 mins
Cooking time: 30 mins

6 tablespoons Dijonnaise (mustard)
125 g (4 oz) softened butter
6 spatchcock or poussin (baby chicken)
6 whole bulbs of garlic
30 large, flat Italian beans

Pumpkin Puree
1 kg (2 lb) butternut pumpkin
2 tablespoons butter
salt and freshly
ground pepper

Wine:
Choose a lighter style of red wine, such as pinot noir, an Italian varietal like sangiovese, or a chardonnay to balance the buttery flavours of this dish, with just a little kick from the mustard.

Preheat oven to moderately hot, 200°C (400°F, Gas Mark 6). Combine equal quantities of mustard and butter. Using your fingers, force about 2 tablespoons of this mixture under the skin and over the breast of each spatchcock. Place in oven with 1 whole bulb of garlic per person—slice off the top before cooking to reveal the garlic cloves.

Meanwhile, bake, steam or microwave pumpkin until very soft. Mash with butter, salt and pepper, adding a little more butter or cream, milk or stock if it is too stiff.

After 20 minutes, check if spatchcock are cooked by piercing the thickest part of thighs. If juices run clear, they are cooked. Otherwise return to the oven for another 5–10 minutes. Remove with the garlic to a warm plate to rest, upending the spatchcock so that any juices inside run into the baking dish. Boil the contents of the baking pan over high heat while you cook some Italian beans in salted boiling water for a few minutes.

To serve, place a mound of pumpkin puree on each plate. Place the beans, spatchcock and garlic (which will now be sweet and soft and squeeze easily out of its skin) on the plate and drizzle with pan juices.

Spiced Quail with Nam Jim

Nam jim is a versatile accompaniment for plain grilled chicken, lamb or even fish. It is sensational with quail.

Serves: 6 as an entree or part of a larger meal, 3 as a main course.
Preparation time: 10 mins + 1 hour marinating
Cooking time: 20 mins + 5 mins resting

6 quail
banana leaf, to serve

Marinade

¼ cup (2 fl oz) kecap manis (sweet Indonesian soy sauce)
1 tablespoon Thai fish sauce (nam pla)
2 tablespoons rice wine vinegar or mirin
2 tablespoons ground coriander (cilantro)
1 teaspoon ground cumin
5 pieces star anise
1 bunch coriander (cilantro), leaves

Nam Jim

4 large coriander roots
3 red chillies, seeded
15 eschalots
4 cloves garlic
155 g (5 oz) palm sugar (or brown sugar)
¾ cup (6 fl oz) fresh lime juice (4–5 limes)
¼ cup (2 fl oz) Thai fish sauce (nam pla)

Combine all marinade ingredients in a large bowl and rub all over the quail. Marinate for at least 1 hour.

Grill quail for about 10 minutes each side, taking care not to burn. Alternatively, cook in a hot oven, 220°–230°C (450°–475°F, Gas Mark 6), for about 20 minutes, or on the barbecue. Rest quail in a warm place for about 5 minutes.

To prepare nam jim, combine coriander, chilli, eschalots, garlic and palm sugar in a food processor, then blend in lime juice and fish sauce. Serve quail on a banana leaf (optional) with rice noodles and nam jim.

Wine:

Choose a soft style of red wine, such as pinot noir, grenache or Italian variety dolcetto.

Moroccan Lamb Kofta on Rosemary Skewers

In the fabulous markets of Morocco I saw huge baskets of spices, roasted and ground fresh each day. The rosemary skewers, though not authentic, look pretty.

Serves: 2–3 or makes 10 balls as finger food
Preparation time: 15 mins + resting
Cooking time: 10 mins

10 rosemary sprigs on firm stems (optional) or bamboo skewers
500 g (1 lb) finely minced lamb
1 small onion, coarsely grated
2 cm (¾ in) piece fresh ginger, peeled and grated
1 teaspoon ground coriander (cilantro)
2 teaspoons ground cumin
grated rind of 1 orange
½ teaspoon paprika
½ teaspoon ground cinnamon
½ teaspoon turmeric
pinch of chilli powder
1 tablespoon finely chopped parsley
1 tablespoon finely chopped coriander
salt and pepper to taste
1 small egg

Yoghurt Sauce
¾ cup (6 fl oz) thick Greek-style yoghurt
1 tablespoon chopped coriander
1 tablespoon chopped mint

Soak rosemary or bamboo skewers in cold water for an hour or so to prevent scorching. Drain. Combine all kofta ingredients in a bowl and mix thoroughly with your hands (alternatively, use a food processor). Ideally, rest mixture in the refrigerator for about an hour for the flavours to develop. (It is also possible to add some cooked rice to the mince mixture.)

Either roll into 6 rissoles or take walnut-size amounts and firmly squeeze into ball shapes around rosemary skewers, 2 per skewer. (For finger food, use small skewers and put only 1 ball on each). Grill, barbecue or pan-fry, turning regularly, until golden, about 10 minutes.

Meanwhile, combine the sauce ingredients. Serve kofta with sauce and couscous, prepared according to directions on packet.

Wine:
Moroccan flavours make a sublime match with cabernet sauvignon but as there is a pinch of chilli, try a cabernet merlot.

Moroccan Lamb Shanks with Quinces

This recipe requires only a little preparation and then no supervision. Put it in the oven overnight or before you go to work and when you come home not only will dinner be cooked but its aroma will waft enticingly through the air. Alternatively you could cook the dish for one and a half to two hours in a moderate oven.

Serves: 8 or 4 very hungry people
Preparation time: 10 mins
Cooking time: Up to 8 hours

4 onions
2 tablespoons olive oil
8 lamb drumsticks (French trimmed lamb shanks)
2 teaspoons turmeric
2 teaspoons cumin
2 teaspoons ground coriander (cilantro)
2 teaspoons cinnamon
salt and freshly ground black pepper
1 tablespoon minced ginger
1 tablespoon minced garlic
1 x 810 g (1¾ lb) tin good quality tomatoes
400 ml (14 fl oz) beef, veal or lamb stock
2 quinces

Couscous

1½ cups (10 oz) couscous
1½ cups (12½ fl oz) boiling chicken stock or water
zest of 1 orange
¼ cup currants
¼ cup finely chopped parsley
⅓ cup toasted flaked almonds

Cut the onions into quarters or eighths and place on the base of an oven tray with a little olive oil. Place in the oven while it heats to 220°C (440°F, Gas Mark 7).

Meanwhile, rub the lamb shanks with the mixed dry spices. When the oven is hot, place the drumsticks in the pan on top of the onion and cook for 15–20 minutes, turning over half way (they can also be placed in a slow cooker). Add the ginger, garlic, tomatoes, stock and the quinces scrubbed, cored and cut into eighths. Cover carefully with a double layer of foil. (You can even seal it with a flour and water paste if you like.) Immediately lower the oven to 80°–100°C (180°–215°F, Gas Mark 1) and leave in the oven for up to 8 hours.

Pour boiling stock or water over couscous, cover and leave 5 mins. Fluff up with a fork and mix through remaining ingredients.

Serve lamb shanks with quinces with couscous.

Wine:

Moroccan spices find a wonderful synergy with cabernet sauvignon and cabernet blends, as long as there is not too much chilli heat.

Lamb Chinese Style

This type of marinade is more usually used with pork, but I just love these sweet, rich flavours with wonderful Australian lamb. The flavour is similar to char siew sauce. You could also cook the lamb, wrapped in foil on the barbecue.

Serves: 6
Preparation time: 10 mins + 24 hours marinading
Cooking time: 45 mins + 10 mins resting

1 butterflied leg of lamb

Marinade
4 cloves garlic, crushed
1 tablespoon sugar
1 tablespoon chopped fresh ginger
2 tablespoons tomato sauce
2 tablespoons soy sauce
2 tablespoons dry sherry
¼ cup (3 tablespoons) hoi sin sauce
1 tablespoon honey
1 teaspoon Chinese five spice powder

Combine marinade ingredients, pour over the meat and marinate for up to 24 hours.

Preheat the oven to 230°C (450°F, Gas Mark 8).

Remove the meat from the marinade and place on a rack in a roasting tin with about 2cm (¾in) hot water in the bottom. This stops the pan from becoming sticky and difficult to wash. Roast for 45 minutes or until cooked, basting several times with the reserved marinade. Alternatively wrap the lamb in foil and cook on the barbecue.

Rest meat for 10 minutes, carve and serve with extra hoi sin sauce.

Cook's note:
The juices from the baking tray can be reduced and used as a sauce.

Wine:
The lamb and the marinade are both sweet, so a red wine with sweet, ripe fruit such as a shiraz is called for, or a grenache.

Lamb Mini-roast with Garlicky White Bean Purée

Try this great meal when you are in a hurry. It looks as if it takes much more care and time than it actually does!

Serves: 2
Preparation time: 5 mins
Cooking time: 30 mins + 5–10 mins resting

1 x 400 g (14 oz) lamb mini-roast (rump or round)
fresh rosemary
2 cloves garlic, crushed
olive oil
1 small can white cannellini beans
zucchini (courgettes), to serve
cherry tomatoes, to serve

Allow one lamb topside roast (weighing around 400 g/ 14 oz) for two people. Calculate the cooking time by allowing 7 minutes per 100 g (3½ oz) for rare, 9 minutes per 100 g (3½ oz) for medium. Sprinkle the lamb with the rosemary and olive oil and place in an oven preheated to 220°C (430°F, Gas Mark 7) and immediately reduce the heat to 200°C (400°F, Gas Mark 6).

While it is cooking, gently sauté one or two crushed cloves of garlic in a little olive oil in a medium pan. Drain and rinse the can of white cannellini beans, add to the garlic and warm them through, then purée in a food processor.

Remove the meat from oven and rest in a warm place for 5–10 minutes before carving. To serve put a mound of white bean purée in the centre of each plate, top with some sliced lamb and drizzle the pan juices over the top.

Serve with a sautéed medley of zucchini in different colours tossed in a pan with cherry tomatoes.

Wine:
Cabernet sauvignon or a blend with this in it such as a cabernet merlot is always good with roast lamb.

Grilled Veal Cutlet with Tomato Alioli

The idea for this sauce came from something I read about a type of mayonnaise or alioli made in Spain where tomato replaces the eggs.

Serves: 6
Preparation time: 10 mins
Cooking time: 30–40 mins

6 desirée potatoes, halved, skin on
fresh rosemary
2 ripe red tomatoes
1 clove garlic
150–200 ml (5–7 fl oz) extra virgin olive oil
6 thick veal cutlets, well trimmed
salad greens, to serve

Pre-heat oven to 200°C (400°F, Gas Mark 6)

Cook the potatoes by par-boiling or microwaving until almost tender. Then roast them in the oven with the rosemary. At the same time, roast the tomatoes in the oven. Remove tomatoes when soft, approximately 15 minutes. Cool a little. Leave potatoes in until golden, approximately 20 minutes more.

Skin the tomatoes and squeeze out the seeds and any excess juice. With the motor running, place the garlic in the food processor or blender, add the tomatoes and mix thoroughly. Then add the extra virgin olive oil, drop by drop until the sauce thickens.

Meanwhile heat a grill pan or barbecue and cook the thick veal cutlets on each side until done, no more than seven minutes on each side.

Serve cutlets with rosemary potatoes, tomato aioli and salad greens.

Wine:
A lighter style of red wine is called for with this lighter meat and the tomatoey sauce. A chambourcin or sangiovese would work well.

Veal with Anchovy Sauce

Nut of veal is traditionally used for Vitello Tonnato. It is less expensive than the fillet and is ideal cooked in this way. Brief cooking also means less shrinkage so the cut is good value. It is a good idea to rinse the anchovies before you use them to remove salt and oil.

Serves: 4–6
Preparation time: 10 mins
Cooking time: 20–30 mins + 10 mins resting

2 tablespoons olive oil
1 nut of veal, from 500 g–1 kg (1–2 1b)
freshly ground black pepper
8 cloves garlic
English spinach, to serve

Sauce

1½ cups (12 fl oz) beef stock
¾ cup (6 fl oz) red wine
6 good quality anchovies, rinsed
2–3 tablespoons thick cream

Celeriac Puree

2 heads celeriac
2 tablespoons (or more) cream

Wine:

Choose a robust red wine with this richly flavoured dish, a cabernet sauvignon, shiraz or rhone-style blend of grenache, shiraz and mourvedre.

Preheat oven to hot, 220°–230°C (450°–475°F, Gas Mark 7). Start the sauce by bringing beef stock and wine to the boil in a saucepan and simmering to reduce.

Pour olive oil all over veal, season with pepper and place in a pan. Place garlic cloves around meat and place pan in the oven for 10 minutes to seal. Reduce heat to slow, 150°C (300°F, Gas Mark 2) and cook for another 10 minutes per 500 g/1 lb (so for 500 g/1 lb nut cook 10 minutes more, for 1 kg/2 lb cook 20 minutes more). Rest meat in the turned-off oven (or another warm place) for at least 10 minutes.

Meanwhile, make celeriac puree. Peel and dice celeriac and cook in boiling, salted water until tender. Drain. Process in food processor with enough cream to make a thick, mousse-like consistency. (If necessary, place in a heatproof container and cover to keep warm.) Do not add any other seasoning at this stage.

When combined beef stock and wine has been reduced to about ¾ cup (6 fl oz), remove from heat. Blend with anchovies. Return to the heat and stir in cream. Taste the sauce—it is unlikely to need more salt. After tasting the sauce, you can decide whether or not the celeriac puree needs seasoning. Slice veal, nap with sauce and serve with celeriac mash, steamed English spinach and roasted garlic cloves from around the veal.

Seared Kangaroo Fillet in a Salad with Moroccan Flavours

Serves: 6
Preparation time: 10 mins
Cooking time: 10–12 mins

olive oil
2 kangaroo strip loin fillets (150 g/5 oz each)

Couscous salad

1 cup (8 fl oz) chicken stock
1 cup (7 oz) instant couscous
2 red chillies, deseeded, finely chopped
2 tablespoons raisins
2 tablespoons parsley, chopped
2 tablespoons toasted pine nuts
2 tablespoons coriander (cilantro), chopped
salt and pepper
2 tablespoons olive oil

Sauce

1 onion, finely chopped
2 cloves garlic, finely chopped
1 large tomato, finely diced
2 teaspoons harissa
2 teaspoons sweet paprika
4 teaspoons cumin
salt and pepper
1 teaspoon sugar
juice of 1 small lemon
100 ml (3½ oz) olive oil
2 tablespoons
¼ cup chopped coriander

Heat the olive oil in a pan until very hot. Quickly sear the kangaroo fillets until they are brown all over. This should take no more than 5 minutes or so but don't overcook as kangaroo is a very lean meat. Remove from the pan and cool.

Pour boiling stock over the couscous, cover and leave 5 minutes to swell. Fluff over with a fork and then combine with chillies, raisins, parsley, pine nuts, coriander, salt, pepper and extra olive oil. Leave to cool.

Make the sauce by gently wilting the onion and garlic in a little olive oil in the same pan in which you browned the roo fillets. Add the tomato and cook a little longer. Stir in all the spices. When well combined, add the lemon juice. Whisk in the olive oil (it may be easier to do this in a jug or deep container). Taste and adjust seasoning if necessary.

Carve the roo into fine slices. Lay flat on a platter and cover with the sauce. Sprinkle with chopped coriander and serve on couscous salad.

Cook's note:
This also works well with beef or lamb.

Wine:
Lots of rich flavours here and a bit of chilli heat so go for a grenache or a shiraz or even a blend where these wines are dominant such as a grenache/shiraz/mourvedre or even shiraz/cabernet.

Spaghetti with Prosciutto and Rocket

The ultimate fast and easy recipe; this is based on a delicious pasta dish I had once in Rome. There smoked marlin was used. As this is hard to get, I have substituted prosciutto. Ask your deli to slice some prosciutto thickly for you.

Serves: 4
Preparation time: 5 mins
Cooking time: 10 mins

300 g spaghetti or other fine pasta
4 slices prosciutto about 1 cm (½ in) wide
extra-virgin olive oil
2 cloves garlic, crushed
1 bunch rocket (arugula)
Parmesan cheese, freshly shaved

Cook the spaghetti or fine pasta in plenty of salted, boiling water in the usual way. Meanwhile, dice the prosciutto.

In another pan, warm some olive oil, add a crushed clove or two of garlic and toss it around with the prosciutto. When the pasta is done, drain it, toss it into the pan with the prosciutto and garlic. Add some leaves of rocket and serve immediately with fresh Parmesan cheese. The heat in the pasta will gently wilt the rocket.

Cook's note:
If you like more liquid with your pasta add a little of the water in which you cooked the pasta, or drizzle with olive oil.

Wine:
The texture of this recipe will match the texture in pinot gris or viognier.

Asian-Style Roast Pork Salad

I love roast pork or suckling pig the way the Chinese do it—my family are all big fans of the crackling and I buy roast pork, for a treat, from my local Asian supermarket. Combined here with salad ingredients, it makes a wonderful dish with great texture and flavour contrasts—and, best of all, it takes hardly any effort.

Serves: 6–8
Preparation time: 10 mins
Cooking time: 5 mins

375 g (12 oz) Chinese roast pork
1 bunch watercress, broken into sprigs
3 cups bean sprouts
½ small Chinese cabbage, shredded
1 red onion, finely sliced

Dressing
2 cloves garlic, crushed
5cm (2in) piece ginger, grated
2 teaspoons Thai sweet chilli sauce (kecap manis)
⅓ cup (2½ fl oz) low-salt soy sauce
⅓ cup (2½ fl oz) peanut oil
2 tablespoons lime juice
2 teaspoons sugar
good pinch Chinese 5 spice powder

Combine dressing ingredients and set aside. Have pork warm or at room temperature—it can be reheated in a moderate oven, 180°–190°C (350°–375°F, Gas Mark 4), so the crackling stays crisp. Toss all salad ingredients together in a large salad bowl and pour dressing over. Serve immediately with the pork.

Wine:
For this dish choose a sauvignon blanc, a dry style of gewürztraminer, riesling or pinot gris.

Pork Fillet with Pistachio and Parsley Pesto

Although I am a little tired of traditional pinenut and basil pesto, I love the different flavours made with other herbs and nuts. This one is a particularly good combination that complements lean pork fillet very well.

Serves: 6
Preparation time: 10 mins
Cooking time: 15 mins

1 tablespoon olive oil
3 pork fillets, about 1 kg (2 lb)
1⅔ cups (13 fl oz) stock
¾ cup (6 fl oz) red wine
mashed potato, to serve
salad greens, to serve

Pistachio and Parsley Pesto

200 g (6½ oz) pistachio nuts in shells or 100 g (3½ oz) pistachio kernels
3 cloves garlic
½ bunch Continental parsley
pinch salt
75 g (2½ oz) fresh parmesan, grated
⅔ cup (5 fl oz) extra virgin olive oil

Cook's note:

Any left over pesto keeps well, covered with olive oil, in the refrigerator.

Wine:

Choose a full-flavoured wine, such as a chardonnay or oaked semillon.

To prepare pesto, shell pistachios and roast briefly in a moderate oven, 180°–190°C (350°–375°F, Gas Mark 4), or cook on high in the microwave for a few minutes until toasted. This develops the flavour of the nuts. When cool, chop in a food processor. Add garlic, parsley and salt and process to a puree. Add parmesan and process to combine. Slowly pour in the oil, a little at a time, until pesto is smooth and well combined (see Cook's note).

To cook pork, heat olive oil in a frying pan and brown fillets, turning so they brown evenly all over. Either lower the heat and continue to cook more gently until cooked through, or place in a hot oven, 220°–230°C (450°–475°F, Gas Mark 7), for 5–10 minutes. Rest for a few minutes in a warm place before carving diagonally into thick slices.

Pour stock and wine into pan in which pork was cooked. Boil vigorously to reduce. Serve pork and pesto with mashed potato and a green salad. Alternatively, serve pork with pasta or noodles in individual bowls, pour over reduced stock, top with sliced pork and a dollop of pesto.

Pad Thai

This is one of the classics of Thai cuisine. Rice noodles are my favourite and I love this combination. Dried shrimp, used as a flavouring ingredient, are available at Asian supermarkets. Fresh prawns or chicken can be substituted for pork.

Serves: 4–6
Preparation time: 10 mins
Cooking time: 12 mins

315 g (10 oz) dried rice noodles
¼ cup (2 fl oz) peanut oil
2 eggs, lightly beaten
1 medium onion, sliced
3 cloves garlic, finely chopped
220 g (7 oz) lean pork (e.g. pork fillet), sliced
2 tablespoons dried shrimp
90 g (3 oz) bean curd, diced
pinch of chilli flakes
¼ cup (2 fl oz) lime juice (1–2 limes)
¼ cup (2 fl oz) Thai fish sauce
2 tablespoons palm sugar (or brown sugar)
1–2 cups (8–16 oz) bean sprouts
50g (1½ oz) roasted, unsalted peanuts, chopped
2 tablespoons garlic chives, chopped
2 tablespoons coriander (cilantro) leaves, chopped

To serve
lime wedges, optional
chilli flakes

Soak rice noodles in hot water for about 10 minutes, or until soft; drain. Heat 1 tablespoon oil in wok over medium heat and scramble the eggs. Remove and set aside. Heat remaining oil and fry onion for 1 minute before adding garlic. Continue to stir-fry until just beginning to brown. Increase heat to high, add pork and cook until pork is cooked through. Add shrimp, bean curd and chilli flakes. Stir through carefully and reduce heat to medium.

Add lime juice, fish sauce and sugar, stirring to dissolve. Add drained noodles and mix through. Add eggs and most of the bean sprouts, peanuts, chives and coriander. Toss all together. Serve immediately, garnished with remaining bean sprouts, peanuts, chives and coriander. Serve with lime wedges and a pile of chilli flakes.

Wine:
Choose a white wine with some citrus character with this dish—perhaps a riesling, or unoaked chardonnay, or a young semillon.

Spicy Pork Stir-fry with Noodles

Curry pastes are a boon to the home cook who does not have the time to roast and grind spices. It's a great way to enjoy authentic flavours. But we Australians are great adaptors and so I have used tom yum paste not for soup, but in a stir-fry. It gives a delicious and unusual flavour.

Serves: 4
Preparation time: 5 mins + marinating
Cooking time: 10 mins

625 g (1 ¼ lb) lean diced pork
30–60 g (1–2 oz) red curry paste
30–60 g (1–2 oz) tom yum soup paste
1 tablespoon peanut oil
½ cup sliced green onions (shallots)
½ cup (4 fl oz) chicken stock
½ cup peanuts, preferably dry-roasted
½ bunch coriander (cilantro), chopped
egg noodles (to serve)

Mix pork with red curry paste and tom yum paste and leave to marinate, preferably for 1–2 hours.

Heat oil in a wok until very hot and, making sure your exhaust fan is on, quickly sear and begin to cook pork, in 2 batches, for 2 minutes each batch. Return it all to the wok and add green onions. Cook about 1 minute longer, but don't let it burn. Add stock and cook until pork is cooked through. Throw in peanuts and coriander and stir through. Serve pork over egg noodles.

Cook's note:
This dish is HOT! To reduce the heat, decrease the quantity of spice paste you use.

Wine:
Choose a wine with fruit sweetness to counteract the heat of the chilli, perhaps a sauvignon blanc, gewürztraminer, riesling, pinot noir or grenache.

Corned Beef with Horseradish Cream and Olive Mash

Corned beef is not fast but it sure is easy and takes little preparation time. It's something that lots of people love but are afraid to cook.

Serves: 4–6
Preparation time: 5 mins
Cooking time: 60 mins

1 piece corned beef, approximately 1 kg (2 lb)
1 onion stuck with a dozen cloves
¼ cup (2 fl oz) vinegar
2 tablespoons sugar
2 bay leaves
4–6 potatoes
extra virgin olive oil
salt and pepper
½ cup black olives, sliced

Sauce
1 cup (8 fl oz) chicken stock
½ cup (4 fl oz) white wine
½ cup (4 fl oz) cream
1 heaped teaspoon horseradish

Cover the corned beef with fresh cold water to which the onion stuck with a dozen cloves, vinegar, sugar and bay leaves have been added. Bring to the boil and simmer for an hour or so for a small piece, longer for a large one. (Your butcher will advise you or packaged corned beef from the supermarket will have cooking times on it.) Meanwhile peel and boil the potatoes until very soft.

For the Sauce:
Boil chicken stock, white wine, cream and horseradish over high heat until well reduced and thickened.

Once the potatoes are done, drain and mash with extra virgin olive oil, salt and pepper. When fluffy, fold in the sliced black olives.

To serve, slice the beef across the grain, pour over some of the sauce and serve with these delicious potatoes.

Wine:
The soft flavour of a pinot noir or grenache are best here.

Chinese Roast Duck Salad

Chinese roast duck, now easily available, is one of my all-time favourites. Put it on rice crackers for a canapé, curry it or just eat it plain. Here it is in a salad.

I prefer to buy the duck whole or in halves and bone it myself before chopping. If you don't mind the bones, the vendor will chop it for you. It is most delicious warm so use it immediately or place the chopped duck, skin side down, in a fry pan over a gentle to medium heat. This warms the duck and renders some of the fat so that it doesn't go on your hips!

Serves: 4–6
Preparation time: 10 mins
Cooking time: 5 mins

2 cups mixed green leaves
1 punnet snow pea (mangetout) shoots
1 avocado, sliced
½ bunch green onions (shallots), chopped
½ red papaya or paw paw
½ cup (4 fl oz) shelled pistachio nuts
1 Chinese roast duck, warm

Dressing
1 teaspoon sesame oil
50 ml olive oil (preferably flavoured with garlic)
½ teaspoon grated ginger
1 teaspoon Thai sweet chilli sauce
(kecap manis)
salt and pepper

Combine the dressing ingredients. Place some mixed green leaves and snow pea shoots into a deep bowl. Add the avocado, green onions, papaya, pistachio nuts and finally the duck. Drizzle the dressing over the salad and serve immediately.

Wine:
Pinot noir is a natural match with duck, but as this is a salad a pinot gris can work well too.

In 2004 I was one of six "Great Women Chefs of Australia" to cook a charity dinner.

My first visit to London where I lived from 1979–80.

With my son Blair and daughter Lucy.

I am a judge of the Lexus Young Chef of the Year. This photo was taken at the 2007 awards.

John, my partner and I, celebrating at L'Astrance in Paris, one of the world's great restaurants.

SWEET PLATES

Tiny Passionfruit Butter Tarts

These make a lovely change from larger lemon-curd tarts. They make a great finalé to a cocktail party.

Makes: 24 +
Preparation time: 25 mins
Cooking time: 10 mins

Sweet Shortcrust Pastry
1 cup (4 oz) plain flour
½ cup (1¾ oz) icing sugar
pinch salt
2½ tablespoons (2½ oz) unsalted butter, chilled and diced
2 egg yolks or 1 whole egg
¼ teaspoon vanilla essence

Passionfruit Butter
pulp of 10 passionfruit (about ¾ cup)
½ cup (3½ oz) caster sugar
2½ tablespoons (2½ oz) unsalted butter
1 whole egg
3 egg yolks

Wine:
These come at the end of the meal so serve with coffee or a dessert wine like a botrytis semillon.

This pastry is very 'short' and quite delicious. However, it is difficult to handle on a hot day because of the high butter content, so try to keep everything cold. Good quality commercial pastry could be substituted but the effort in making it yourself will be well rewarded.

To make the pastry, put the flour, sugar and salt into the bowl of your food processor. Add butter and combine briefly using the on/off or pulse switch on your processor. This avoids over-processing, which will toughen the pastry. Add the egg yolks and vanilla essence at the end and process just enough to combine. You may need to add a tablespoon or so of cold water if the mixture does not come together.

Pre-heat the oven to 200°C (400°F, Gas Mark 6)

Roll out the pastry thinly (this may be easier in between two sheets of baking paper). Cut with a small crouton or scone cutter. Line tiny tart tins with the pastry and prick it well with a fork. Place the tarts in the freezer for 15 mins or until frozen. This can be done a day or two in advance. Bake in the hot oven until brown, approximately 10 minutes.

To make the filling, combine all ingredients in a saucepan. Cook gently, stirring all the time until it thickens. Push through a sieve to remove the seeds. Return a few seeds to the mixture, so that it is obvious that it is passionfruit and not just lemon! Cool. Store in the fridge until needed.

Dust the tart shells with icing sugar and pipe or spoon in the filling.

Lemon or Lime Tart

Serves: 6–8
Preparation time: 15 mins
Cooking time: 45 mins

Pastry

1¼ cups (7 oz) plain flour
½ cup (3 oz) icing sugar
3 tablespoons unsalted butter, diced
1 egg
1 tablespoon cold water (optional)

Filling

4 eggs
⅓ cup (2½ oz) caster sugar
1¼ cup (10¼ fl oz)) cream
juice of 2–3 lemons or limes
icing sugar

whipped or thick cream, to serve

Cook's note:

Pricking and freezing the pastry is a shortcut to blind baking where normally baking paper is put over the pastry in the tin, weighted down with beans or rice, and then baked in the oven for about 10 mins before the paper and weights are removed for a final 5 minutes or so of baking. Either method is necessary to ensure a crisp based tart.

Wine:

These lovely lemon flavours are best with a wine with some sweet citrus flavours like a late-picked or cordon-cut riesling.

For the pastry, put the flour and icing sugar in a food processor and combine for a few seconds. Add the butter and process until the mixture resembles breadcrumbs. Add the egg. Process, stopping as soon as the dough forms into balls and clings around blade. If this doesn't happen, add a little chilled water until it does. Remove, wrap in plastic wrap and refrigerate for at least one hour; the pastry can be left overnight.

Preheat the oven to 200°C (400°F, Gas Mark 6).

Roll out the dough on a lightly floured board and line a high-sided flan tin approximately 26cm (10 in) across. Press the pastry gently into the tin and use a rolling pin to trim the excess from the perimeter. Prick all over, including the sides, with a fork. Place in the freezer for at least 15 minutes or until frozen (again, overnight is fine). Cook in the oven for 10–15 minutes until it is golden brown.

Reduce the oven temperature to 170°C (345°F, Gas Mark 2–3).

To make the filling, beat the eggs and caster sugar together until pale. Pour in the cream and, finally, the juice. Pour immediately into the prepared pastry base and bake until it is just set, about 25-30 minutes. Cool.

Dust with icing sugar and serve with whipped or thick cream.

Lemon Polenta Cake with Lemon Mascarpone

Polenta cakes have a long tradition in Italy. This recipe comes from my friend Luci Lothringer, who adapted it from one her mother used to make.

Serves: 12–16
Preparation time: 10 mins
Cooking time: 90 mins

¾ cup (6 fl oz) lemon juice (3–4 lemons)
500 g (1 lb) unsalted butter, softened
500 g (1 lb) caster sugar
6 eggs
½ teaspoon vanilla essence
rind of 4 lemons
410 g (13 oz) almond meal
280 g (9 oz) polenta (cornmeal)
1½ teaspoon baking powder
pinch salt

Lemon Mascarpone

2 tablespoons brandy
1 cup (7 oz) caster sugar
rind of 1 lemon
¼ cup (2 fl oz) lemon juice
¾ cup (6 fl oz) milk, or ⅓ cup (2 fl oz) dry white wine
500g (1lb) mascarpone

Wine

Choose a late-picked or botrytis riesling to serve with this delicious cake.

Zest or grate rind of 2 lemons and reserve. Juice them plus 1 or 2 more to get ¾ cup juice. You will need five or six juicy lemons for this recipe, and two more if you decorate with shreds of rind as suggested.

Preheat oven to moderately slow, 160°C (325°F, Gas Mark 3). Grease a 26cm (10in) springform cake tin with extra light olive oil spray and line base with baking paper.

Cream butter and sugar until pale, then slowly beat in eggs, one at a time. Stir in vanilla, lemon rind and juice, then fold in almond meal, polenta, baking powder and salt. Pour into cake tin and bake for 30 minutes. Cover with foil and bake for 1 hour more, or until a skewer inserted into the centre comes out clean. Remove from oven, cool. Serve with lemon mascarpone and glazed lemon rind.

To make lemon mascarpone, combine all ingredients in a food processor, taking care not to overbeat.

To make glazed lemon rind bring ½ cup (4 fl oz) water to the boil with ½ cup (4 oz) sugar, add the shredded rind of 2 lemons and simmer for 10 minutes, or until rind softens and is glazed with sugar.

Swiss Cottage Library - Kiosk 4

Thank you for using self service

Borrowed Items 28/08/2016 14:24
XXXXXXXXX9273

Item Title	Due Date
* Lyndey Milan, the best collection : fast, fabulous food	22/09/2016
The Paleo chef : quick, flavourful Paleo meals for eating well	03/09/2016
Complete yoga workbook : a practical approach to healing common ailments with yoga	12/09/2016
The overnight diet : start losing weight tonight, and keep it off permanently	12/09/2016
10 secrets for success and inner peace [sound recording] /]	12/09/2016

* Indicates items borrowed today

Free e books to download from Camden libraries

www.camden.gov.uk/ebooks

F audio books to download from Camden

gov.uk/audiobooks
enjoy!

Orange Bread and Butter Pudding

Fans of the English TV series Pie in the Sky *will know why I've developed this recipe. Policeman and chef Henry Crabbe hot on the tail of two thieving old ladies made sure he found out the secret ingredient of their bread & butter pudding before he nabbed them! I share my version of it with you.*

Serves: 6
Preparation time: 10 mins
Cooking time: 30–35 mins

10 slices white bread, approximately
butter, softened
¼ cup good-quality orange marmalade
2 eggs
2 tablespoons vanilla sugar
250 ml (8 fl oz) cream
250 ml (8 fl oz)milk
¼ cup sultanas

Preheat the oven to 190°C (375°F, Gas Mark 5).

Cut the crusts from the bread. Spread with the butter and marmalade. Cut in half diagonally and place in a flat dish or tray.

Whisk together the eggs, vanilla sugar, cream and milk. Pour over bread and soak for 5–10 mins but not so long the bread starts to fall apart.

Arrange bread decoratively in a greased oven-proof dish, overlapping the slices.

Sprinkle with sultanas. Pour over remaining custard mixture.

Bake in the oven for 30–35 minutes, reducing the heat or covering with foil if the top becomes too brown.

Serve cut in wedges with thick cream.

Wine:

The rich orange fruit flavours of a botrytis semillon will fit best here, finding similar notes in the orange marmalade.

Cook's note:

If you stand the bread slices upwards as pictured soak the bread well and then spoon or brush some of the custard mixture over the bread which is elevated above the mixture.

Poached Peaches

Poached peaches, nectarines or other stone-fruits make one of the simplest and most delicious desserts. The skins give the poaching syrup a wonderful pink colour and they slip off easily after cooking.

Serves: 4
Preparation time: Nil
Cooking time: 20 mins

1 cup (7 oz) sugar
1 cup (8 fl oz) water
1 cup (8 fl oz) sparkling or white wine
4 whole perfect peaches
thick cream, to serve

Place sugar, water and wine in a saucepan and stir to dissolve sugar. Add peaches and bring slowly to the boil. Simmer for about 15 minutes, or until peaches are softening but not mushy. Cool in the liquid. Remove peaches and slip off skins. Pour poaching liquid over fruit and serve with thick cream.

Cook's note:

For a truly sensational sorbet, puree poached peaches with their poaching liquor. Freeze and, when solid, cut into chunks and process in a food processor until smooth. Refreeze. Each peach, with poaching liquid, makes about 4 scoops of sorbet.

Wine:

The peaches are not overly sweet, so sip on a sparkling wine with residual sugar.

Another fundraiser where food media cooked and served the food with Suzzane Gibbs and Sue Jenkins.

Stone-Fruit Galette

Adapt this basic recipe to any fruit that is in season. In summer, it's a wonderful opportunity to use peaches and nectarines. At other times of year, use pears or apples.

Serves: 4–6
Preparation time: 15 mins
Cooking time: 15–18 mins

1 packet filo pastry
3 tablespoons melted butter
2 or 3 peaches or 3 or 4 nectarines
1 tablespoon sugar

Preheat the oven to 200°C (400°F, Gas Mark 6).

Have a damp tea towel or cloth ready when working with filo pastry, to prevent it getting brittle.

Unroll the pastry carefully, remove two sheets and brush with butter. Place another two sheets on top and repeat the process until there are ten layers of pastry. (Usually each sheet is brushed with butter, but I find this unnecessary for crisping the filo and leaving it out also reduces the fat content.)

Cut the pastry in half lengthwise and then into six or eight pieces horizontally, so that you end up with twelve or sixteen pieces. This will depend on what size you would like the finished product to be. They can also be cut quite small and served as finger food at the end of a cocktail party.

Peel the peaches carefully (there is no need to peel the nectarines), slice thinly and layer slices on the pastry. Brush the top with butter, sprinkle with sugar and bake until golden, around 15–18 minutes.

Wine:
A late-picked riesling or semillon, or a sparkling wine with residual sugar is the best bet.

Baked Coconut Custard with Mango

Everyone loves crème brulée. Here there's no toffee on top, instead toasted shredded coconut and the custard itself is made with coconut milk. This will not be as silky smooth as a crème brulée but the flavour is perfect for after an Asian-influenced main course.

Serves: 6
Preparation time: 10 mins
Cooking time: 65 mins + chilling

3 cups (24 fl oz) coconut cream
6 egg yolks
1½ tablespoons caster sugar
120 g (4 oz) shredded coconut
fresh mango to serve

Preheat the oven to 150°C (300°F, Gas Mark 2).

Scald the coconut cream by heating either in a saucepan or in the microwave. Beat together the egg yolks and caster sugar. When thick and creamy, whisk in the coconut cream. Pour into six ramekins.

Bake in a bain-marie (hot-water bath) in the oven for 1 hour. Refrigerate to cool and set. Meanwhile toast the shredded coconut by placing in a 180°C (350°F, Gas Mark 4) oven for 5 minutes.

To serve, cut the mango cheeks and invert. Top the custards with toasted coconut and place on a plate. Place mangoes to one side.

Wine:
The richer flavours here need a richer dessert wine like a botrytis semillon.

Warm Winter Fruit Salad

Perhaps not strictly speaking fast and easy in terms of cooking time, but certainly in preparation—and worth the wait with the wonderful aromas that emanate! One to enjoy during cold weather using whatever fruits are in season.

Serves: 6
Preparation time: 10 mins
Cooking time: 90 mins

½ cup (4 oz) brown sugar
juice of 1 lemon
½ cinnamon stick
½ vanilla bean
½ teaspoon cardamom seeds
1 quince
50 g (1¾ oz) dried apricots
6 dried figs
10 fresh cumquats
2 pears
1 tangelo or large mandarin, segmented
6 fresh dates
1–2 tablespoons brandy
clear apple juice (optional)

Combine 1 cup (8 fl oz) water with the sugar and stir over a medium heat until the sugar dissolves. Add the lemon juice, cinnamon, vanilla bean split in half and cardamom seeds.

Peel the quince, cut in half and then into thirds or quarters, depending on size, leaving the core intact to aid thickening. Add this to the syrup. Add enough water to just cover the fruit and return to the simmer. Cover with a cartouche (round of baking paper) weighed down with a saucer and leave to simmer, stirring occasionally for half an hour or so. This ensures the quince remains submerged and cooks evenly.

Then, add apricots, figs and cumquats, and simmer for another half an hour. Add the pears cut into eighths, tangelo and dates, and simmer for a final half hour with a splash or two of brandy and, if necessary, top up the liquid with some clear apple juice.

To serve, remove the quince and cut away the core. Serve with the remaining salad and syrup in a bowl with some thickened cream. Delicious warm, at room temperature or chilled.

Wine:
Try an oloroso sherry with this, it is sweeter in style yet not cloying.

Cook's note:
This is also delicious served with thick yoghurt for breakfast.

Caramelised Apple Cake

The use of spices in this cake is optional. If you prefer your cake plain, leave them out. The addition of caramel makes a delicious, gooey cake.

Serves: 8
Preparation time: 10 mins
Cooking time: 55–60 mins

125 g (4 oz) butter
⅔ cup (5 oz) caster sugar
1 teaspoon grated lemon rind
2 eggs
1 cup (5 oz) self-raising flour
½ cup (4 oz) plain flour
½ teaspoon ground nutmeg
½ teaspoon ground cinnamon
½ teaspoon ground ginger
½ cup (4 fl oz) thick sour cream
¼ cup (2 fl oz) milk
2 or 3 apples
½ cup (4 fl oz) purchased caramel sauce
cream or ice-cream, to serve

Preheat oven to moderately slow, 160°C (325°F, Gas Mark 3). Grease a 23cm (9in) springform cake tin.

Cream butter, sugar and lemon rind until light and fluffy. Add eggs, one at a time, combining thoroughly after each addition. Beat in the flours and spices (if using), add cream and milk and beat again to a smooth batter. Spread half the mixture over base of prepared tin.

Meanwhile, peel, quarter and core apples and slice thinly. Layer half over the cake mixture. Drizzle with half the caramel sauce. Top with remaining cake mixture and apples. Bake for about 45 minutes. Drizzle with remaining caramel sauce and return to the oven for 10–15 minutes, or until cooked. Stand in the pan for 5 minutes, then remove the springform sides and cool on the base.

Serve warm with cream or ice-cream.

Drink:
This cake is sticky and lush and it is best served with good strong coffee.

Summer Pudding

Summer pudding is the highlight of British cuisine. It is also one recipe that translates well to our Australian climate. Frozen berries work well too.

Serves: 6
Preparation time: 10 mins + overnight resting
Cooking time: 10 mins

1 kg (2 lb) mixed berries, such as strawberries, raspberries, blueberries, boysenberries, youngberries, cranberries, mulberries
½ cup (4 oz) caster sugar
1–2 tablespoons water
12–14 slices day-old white bread

Wine:
As this is not overly sweet, a sparking rosé with a little residual sugar is delightful, or else a moscato will match well.

This recipe can either be made as one large pudding or individual ones in small ramekins.

Pick over the berries and rinse with water. Cut any large berries, such as strawberries, into smaller pieces. Place in a saucepan with the sugar and water. Simmer for about 5 minutes, stirring occasionally, until the fruit softens, releasing their juice.

Remove the crusts from the bread. If you are making one large pudding, cut one slice into a circular shape to fit the bottom of a 1½ l (3 pint) pudding basin. Line the basin or individual ramekins with bread, trimming it so that it fits snugly. There should be some slices left to cover the fruit.

Ladle the fruit and enough juice to moisten the bread into the moulds, reserving a little of the juice. Cover with bread and weight the top with a plate plus something heavy on top. Leave at least overnight, or even for a couple of days.

Shortly before serving, unmould the puddings and baste any white patches of bread with the reserved juice.

I have even frozen this pudding successfully!

Cheat's Berry Brulée

Forget heating cream and egg yolks and hoping that they don't curdle. Try this instead. You can follow your taste and use any combination you like, or these quantities.

Serves: 6
Preparation time: 5–10 mins
Cooking time: 5 mins

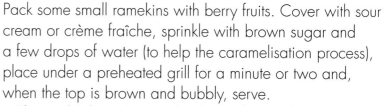

3 punnets Berry Fruits in Season eg blueberries, strawberries, raspberries, blackberries
300 g (10 oz) sour cream or crème fraîche
6 tablespoons brown sugar

Pack some small ramekins with berry fruits. Cover with sour cream or crème fraîche, sprinkle with brown sugar and a few drops of water (to help the caramelisation process), place under a preheated grill for a minute or two and, when the top is brown and bubbly, serve.

This method can be used with any fruit and you may care to serve some extra fruit on the side. If you prepare the ramekins in advance and rest in the fridge prior to caramelising, which is one of the attractions of this dish, don't bother sprinkling with water, as the sugar will melt on the sour cream anyway.

Wine:
The sweet flavours of a late-picked riesling or semillon will work here or even a richer botrytised wine.

Berries remind me of Christmas. I always loved a wonderful charity event, 'Bollinger on the Beach', especially Santa's arrival by boat.

Plum Clafoutis

Clafoutis is a traditional French dish that consists of a batter poured over fruit, usually cherries. Plums make a pleasant alternative, and the brandy and flaked almonds give the batter a lift.

Serves: 8
Preparation time: 10 mins
Cooking time: 45 mins

750 g (1½ lb) plums
½ cup (2½ oz) flour
½ cup (3½ oz) caster sugar
pinch of salt
4 eggs
1 cup (8 fl oz) milk
2 tablespoons brandy
2 tablespoons flaked almonds
extra sugar
cream, to serve

Preheat the oven to 180°C (350°F, Gas Mark 4)
Place the plums in a large saucepan of boiling water. Simmer for 2–3 minutes until just tender. Drain, then plunge into cold water to cool. Cut the plums in half, remove the stems and stones and transfer to a lightly buttered baking dish. If fresh plums are not available, you can use good quality tinned plums—Australian of course!

Place flour, sugar and salt in a bowl or food processor. Beat the eggs in, one at a time, then add half the milk and beat for 5 minutes. Stir in the remaining milk and brandy. Pour mixture over the plums. Sprinkle with flaked almonds. Bake for 40–45 minutes. Sprinkle with extra sugar and serve hot with cream.

Variation:
Apricots or peaches can be substituted for plums.

Wine:
"Sticky" or dessert wines are usually made from late-picked or botrytised riesling or semillon. Both work well here.

Rhubarb Tarte Tatin

I love a good tarte tatin, especially made with pear or quince, but who has time to make one? This simple method is devastatingly delicious!

Serves: 6
Preparation time: 10 mins
Cooking time: 25 mins

1 cup (8 oz) sugar
⅓ cup (2 fl oz) water
¼ cup (2 fl oz)
Grand Marnier or Cointreau
1 bunch rhubarb, cut into
10cm (4in) lengths
1 tablespoon sugar, extra
1 or 2 sheets butter puff pastry
thick cream, to serve

Preheat oven to hot, 220°–230°C (450°–475°F, Gas Mark 7). Make a caramel by heating sugar and water over high heat until medium caramel colour (about 10 minutes). Stir before it comes to the boil to dissolve the sugar, but not after it has come to the boil. Remove from heat and immediately thin with Grand Marnier. (Take care as it may splutter!)

Pour into greased ovenproof pan or dish – I use an oval 22 x 36cm (9 x 14in) but a slab pan, 20 x 30cm (8 x 12in), works well, too. Add rhubarb and sprinkle with extra sugar. Cut the puff pastry sheet to fit the pan and place on the rhubarb. Cook in oven for 12–15 minutes or until pastry is golden.

Remove from oven and rest for 5 minutes. Drain any excess juice released by the rhubarb into a jug and use separately as sauce. Carefully place a board over the entire dish and invert quickly. Cut into slices and serve with thick cream and reserved rhubarb juice.

Wine:
Choose a fresh, fruity style of dessert wine, such as a late-picked riesling or moscato.

Baked Quinces with Almond Tuiles

While this is very fast and easy to prepare, it does take a while in the oven, but your patience will be well rewarded.

Makes: ½–1 quince per person (12–16 large tuiles)
Preparation time: 10 mins
Cooking time: 90 mins

6 large or 12 small quinces
1 teaspoon butter per quince
2 tablespoons sugar per quince
250 g (8 oz) mascarpone or thick cream

Almond Tuiles
2 egg whites
¼ cup (1¾ oz) vanilla sugar
⅓ cup (1¾ oz) flour
2 tablespoons butter, melted
3 tablespoons flaked almonds

Wine:
These rich, luscious flavours cry out for a similarly luscious wine, so try a botrytis semillon.

Preheat the oven to 200°C (400°F, Gas mark 6). Wash the quinces well. Cut them in half along the core and remove the cores and seeds using a sharp, strong knife. Put each quince half, cut side up, on some foil. Top with a sliver of butter and about 2 tablespoons of sugar per quince (or more to taste, quinces are quite sharp). Wrap up the quinces firmly and place in a baking dish, still with the cut side up. Bake for at least an hour and a half or until tender.

To make the tuiles, combine all ingredients. This mixture can be frozen, but it should be brought back to room temperature before use. Place spoonfuls of the mixture on greased paper or silicone-lined trays, sprinkle with flaked almonds and work into large circles with the back of a spoon.

Cook for a short time at 200°C (400°F, Gas mark 6) until golden brown. Remove and drape them immediately over a French-bread tin so that they curl. If the tuiles harden while flat, simply pop them back in the oven to warm so they become pliable again.

Store in an airtight container.

Serve the quince with marscapone or thick cream and the almond tuiles.

Gratinéed Fruit

This recipe includes that old-fashioned favourite, zabaglione. Put it over any seasonal fruit and glaze for an updated approach.

Serves: 4
Preparation time: 5 mins
Cooking time: 10 mins

fresh fruit, such as strawberries or mangoes

Zabaglione
2 egg yolks
2–3 tablespoons marsala
2 tablespoons caster sugar
zest of a lemon

Wine:
As this is both sweet and frothy, drink a sweeter style of sparkling wine.

Put all the zabaglione ingredients in the top of a double boiler, you can put them straight in a saucepan if you are careful. Beat them together with a balloon whisk over gentle heat until the whole thing has trebled in volume and is light and frothy throughout.

Put the fresh fruit into ramekins and top with the zabaglione. Pop under the griller until brown. Be careful not to burn it.

There's always time to party!
This time with chef Tetsuya Wakuda

Honeyed Figs

The number of figs you will need for this recipe will depend on their size.

Serves: 4
Preparation time: 5 mins
Cooking time: 6 mins

1 tablespoon butter
8 figs
4 slices brioche, from a whole loaf
honey
250 g (8 oz) mascarpone or thick cream

Melt enough butter to cover base of the frypan. Cut or tear the figs in half and cook them, cut side down, until golden brown, turning occasionally. Meanwhile toast and butter the slices of brioche. Drizzle honey over the top of the figs and allow it to bubble up. Remove from heat.

Serve figs on or beside the toasted brioche with mascarpone or thick cream.

Cook's note:
Tearing the figs gives an interesting appearance. They can also be placed under the griller, cut side up and then drizzled with honey.

Wine:
Match the honey intensity here with a late picked or cordon cut riesling or semillon

Coeur à la Crème

This is an oldie, but a goodie, a great dessert for lovers. You need perforated heart-shaped moulds as the creme must drain overnight. Lining the moulds with muslin gives an attractive texture to the hearts and also makes them easier to turn out. For a sharper flavour, use half yoghurt and half cream.

Makes: 6 (or 8 with slightly smaller hearts)
Preparation time: 15 mins + overnight chilling
Cooking time: Nil

250 g (8 oz) mascarpone
1¼ cups (½ pint) thickened cream
1 tablespoon vanilla sugar
1 tablespoon Cognac,
Grand Marnier or Cointreau

Berry Purée
250 g (8 oz) berries, e.g. strawberries
or raspberries
1 tablespoon caster sugar or more, to taste
250 g (8 oz) berries, extra, for decoration
mint leaves

Line heart-shaped moulds with wet muslin. Blend mascarpone with cream (or cream and yoghurt), sugar and liqueur, taking care not to overbeat. Fill prepared moulds, place on a tray and leave to drain in the refrigerator for several hours, preferably overnight.

Purée berries with sugar and spoon a little onto individual serving plates. Unmould hearts on top, removing the muslin once the hearts are in place, and decorate with extra berries and mint leaves.

Wine:
Choose a rich, full-bodied dessert wine, such as a botrytis semillon or riesling.

Sticky Toffee Pudding

I'm not sure where this recipe started, but is certainly Australian and become very popular. Suddenly it seemed to be everywhere. It remains a favourite café item.

Serves: 8–10
Preparation time: 5 mins
Cooking time: 30 mins

185 g (6½ oz) stoned dates
1 cup (8 fl oz) water
1 level teaspoon bicarbonate of soda
2 tablespoons butter
2 eggs
¾ cup (6½ oz) sugar
1¼ cups (6½ oz) self-raising flour
¼ teaspoon vanilla essence
thick cream, to serve

Sauce

⅞ cup (5 oz) brown sugar
⅔ cup (5 fl oz) cream
½ cup (4 oz) butter
½ teaspoon vanilla essence

Preheat the oven to 190°C (375°F, Gas Mark 5).
To make the pudding, cook the dates in water until they reach a jammy consistency, stirring frequently to break them up. Beat in the remaining ingredients and mix well. Butter and flour a deep oblong baking tray, and pour in mixture. Bake on the centre shelf of the oven for 25 minutes or until pudding is cooked.

To make the sauce, place all the sauce ingredients in a pan, bring to boil and boil for 5 minutes.

To serve, cut the pudding into wedges and serve with the sauce and thick cream.

Wine:

The wonderful caramel flavours are so intense this could go with a liqueur or just a cup of coffee.

A Food Media Club Christmas happy snap with old mate Peter Howard. We are both past presidents of the club.

With chef Matt Moran at the launch of Tasting Success, a female chef mentoring program which I helped initiate, of which I am now patron.

On the set of Mornings with Kerri-Anne, where I cook weekly.

CHOCOLATE PLATES

Chocolate Plates

Chocolate Beignets

This marvellous recipe comes from Sydney caterer Belinda Franks, who wowed cocktail parties with this chocolate finale for a long time.

Makes: 25
Preparation time: 10 mins + freezing time
Cooking time: 10 mins

125 g (4 oz) plain flour
25 g (¾ oz) cocoa powder
pinch of salt
25 g (¾ oz) sugar
1 egg
½ cup (4 fl oz) sparkling wine
25 g (¾ oz) melted butter
light-flavoured vegetable oil, for deep-frying

Ganache
5 tablespoons (3 fl oz) cream
50 g (3 oz) butter
250 g (8 oz) dark Belgian chocolate, grated

Make ganache first, by boiling cream and pouring over butter and grated chocolate. Stir over hot water in a double boiler until chocolate is melted and smooth. Cool. Cover with cling film and refrigerate until set. Using a 2cm (¾in) melon baller, shape ganache into balls and freeze.

For beignet batter, sieve dry ingredients. Add egg and wine, whisking until smooth, then incorporate melted butter. The batter should be fairly thick. It is better to try this recipe with the batter a bit too thick and add extra wine if necessary. Do not refrigerate the batter.

Place a ball of ganache on a fork and dip into batter. Shake off excess, then quickly drop into hot oil for a few seconds. The batter should become crisp and the chocolate inside should be just starting to melt. Cook in batches.

Wine:
This is a big chocolate hit, but also finger food, so enjoy with a sparkling shiraz.

Chocolate Bread and Butter Pudding

For chocoholics this is a variation on an old favourite. I developed this recipe for my cooking segment on Mornings with Kerri-Anne at Easter, using left-over hot cross buns and Easter eggs in place of the fruit loaf and chocolate. It was a hit!

Serves: 6
Preparation time: 20 mins +15 mins resting
Cooking time: 50 mins

1½ cups (12 fl oz) milk
2 cups (1 pint) cream
⅓ cup (2¾ oz) caster sugar
1 vanilla bean or 1 teaspoon vanilla bean paste
4 eggs
200 g (8 oz) Continental fruit loaf, or croissants sliced thickly
100 g (3½ oz) dark eating chocolate, chopped coarsely
ice-cream to serve

Wine:
The chocolate does not dominate here, so a "sticky" dessert wine will be fine.

Preheat the oven to 170°C (340°F, Gas Mark 3).

Combine the milk, cream and sugar in a small saucepan. Split the vanilla bean in half lengthways; scrape seeds into pan then place pod in pan or add vanilla bean paste. Stir frequently until hot then strain (not necessary if using paste) into large heatproof jug and discard pod. (Wash and reserve it for another use.)

Whisk eggs in large bowl and then pour hot milk mixture in, whisking constantly.

Grease a shallow 2 litre (4 pint) ovenproof dish or baking tray and layer fruit loaf and chocolate in it. Pour over the hot milk mixture. Allow to stand for at least 10 minutes so the bread can absorb the custard and it sets a little, which helps to prevent curdling when not cooking it in a hot water bath.

Bake, uncovered for about 45 minutes or until pudding sets. Remove the pudding from the oven and stand 5 minutes before serving.

Serve with ice-cream.

Chocolate Almond Meringue Cake

Although this delicious cake takes a while to cook, the preparation time is minimal and there is no time-consuming icing to do afterwards.

Serves: 8–10
Preparation time: 10 mins
Cooking time: 1½–2 hours

butter or extra light olive oil, to grease
8 egg whites
1½ cups (12 oz) sugar
1 tablespoon Grand Marnier or Cointreau
350 g (12½ oz) dark chocolate, roughly chopped
250 g (8 oz) slivered almonds, toasted
6–8 glacé figs or dried figs cooked in sugar syrup, chopped
zest of 2 oranges
cocoa
whipped cream

Preheat the oven to 165°C (325°F, Gas Mark 2–3). Grease a 25cm (10in) spring-form cake tin with extra light olive oil spray or butter.

Beat the egg whites until stiff, then slowly add the sugar and Grand Marnier or Cointreau. Fold in chocolate, almonds (toasting them first makes them crisper and develops the flavour), figs and orange zest. Place the cake mixture in the tin and bake for 1½–2 hours. Remove from oven, cool and dust with cocoa. Serve with whipped cream.

Wine:
Chocolate has such an intensity of flavour, it can overpower normal dessert wines. A better choice is a liqueured muscat or tokay.

Simple Chocolate Fudge Cake

What a winning recipe this is! Simply mixed in a saucepan, it is the ultimate in ease.

Serves: 6–8
Preparation time: 10 mins
Cooking time: 60 mins

150 g (5 oz) butter
¾ cup lightly packed (5 oz) brown sugar
100 g (3½ oz) dark chocolate
⅓ cup (2¾ fl oz) condensed milk
½ cup (4 fl oz) good quality chocolate sauce
¼ cup (2 fl oz) cream
1 egg
¾ cup (4 oz) self-raising flour
thick cream, to serve

Preheat the oven to 170°C (330°F, Gas Mark 3). Grease and line, or use a non-stick, 20cm (8in) round cake tin.

Melt the butter gently in a saucepan, then add the sugar, chocolate, condensed milk and chocolate sauce. Cook over a low heat until the mixture thickens slightly and the sugar dissolves. Remove from the heat and cool slightly. Combine the cream and egg and add this with the flour to the chocolate mixture. Mix together well and pour into the cake tin. Bake in the oven for 50–60 minutes.

Cool in the tin, then turn out. A non-stick tin gives a wonderful, smooth, glossy finish to this cake, otherwise sprinkle with icing sugar and serve with thick cream.

Wine:
Liqueured muscat, tokay or a rich sparkling shiraz will cut the richness of this cake.

Chocolate Crème Brulée

This is the most luxurious chocolate custard, made that much more special with a traditional brulee toffee.

Serves 6
Preparation time: 10 mins
Cooking time: 45 mins

6 egg yolks
70 g (2½ oz) caster sugar
300 ml (10 fl oz) thickened cream
1 cup (8 fl oz) milk
200 g (8 oz) dark cooking chocolate, chopped
1 tablespoon liqueur eg Tia Maria, Cointreau
3 tablespoons caster sugar, extra

Pre-heat oven to 150°C (300°F, Gas Mark 2).

Whisk egg yolks and sugar until pale, at least 5 minutes.

Place cream, milk, chocolate and liqueur in a small saucepan over medium heat, stirring constantly until the mixture is smooth. Whisk gently (to minimise air bubbles) into the egg yolk mixture and mix well. Strain into a large jug.

Pour into 6 x ½ cup ramekins and place in a baking dish. Place on shelf of oven then pour enough boiling water to come half way up the side of the ramekins.

Bake for 40 mins or until set. Remove and chill in fridge for several hours or overnight.

Just before serving, sprinkle each evenly with extra caster sugar, flick gently with just a few drops of water (to encourage melting), then caramelise the top with a blow torch, brulee iron or by packing the ramekins in a baking tray filled with ice and placing it under pre-heated griller. Allow to cool slightly till caramel layer hardens then serve.

Cook's note:
Although a normal brulée is made entirely with cream, the inclusion of chocolate here means that a combination of milk and cream gives a better consistency.

Wine:
This is a rich, intense dessert and I would drink a cognac or coffee with it!

Chocolate Ganache Tart

Serves: 12
Preparation time: 25 mins + 1½ hours chilling
Cooking time: 15–20 mins

Pastry
1¼ cups (185 g) plain flour
1 tablespoon cocoa
1 tablespoon icing sugar
150 g (5 oz) cold unsalted butter, diced
⅓ cup (2¾ fl oz) sour cream

Ganache
300 ml (10 fl oz) thickened cream
50 g (1¾ oz) butter, diced
300 g (10 oz) dark eating quality chocolate
1 tablespoon Cointreau

cream, ice-cream or thick Greek-style yoghurt,
to serve

For the pastry:

Place flour, sifted cocoa and icing sugar in the bowl of a food processor. Add butter and pulse until the mixture resembles coarse breadcrumbs. Add the sour cream and pulse again just until it forms a ball. Wrap in plastic wrap and refrigerate for 20 minutes at least.

Roll out the dough between two pieces of baking paper to 5mm (¼in) thick and carefully fit into a 23cm (9in measured at base) x 4cm (1½in) deep flan tin with removable base. Make sure the pastry overlaps the edges, trim neatly by running rolling pin around the edge. It will shrink but this is fine. Prick all over with a fork (this helps with blind baking) and place in freezer for 15 minutes or until frozen.

Pre-heat oven to 200°C (400°F, Gas Mark 6). Line frozen pastry with baking paper and pastry weights or dried beans and blind bake for 10–15 minutes, then remove paper and weights and return to oven for another 5 minutes. Make sure the pastry is cooked through and crisp as the tart is not cooked again.

For the Ganache:

Heat cream and butter in a small saucepan and stir until butter melts. Stir in broken or chopped chocolate and stir until melted (this can also be done in the microwave). Stir in Cointreau. Pour into baked tart shell and refrigerate until firm, around one hour.

Continues over page

Chocolate Ganache Tart continued

To serve, place long knife in boiling water and cut small pieces as the tart is very rich. Serve with cream, ice-cream or thick Greek-style yoghurt.

Cook's note:

This pastry is very short so it shrinks. I have used a 4cm (1½in) deep flan tin to accommodate this. You would not want the ganache this thick anyway as it would be too rich. If you use a shallower flan tin, make sure you overlap the pastry over the sides to allow for shrinkage.

Wine:

This is all about chocolate and is so intensely flavoured that it would overwhelm all but the most intensely flavoured wines, so my choice would be a full-bodied sparkling red wine. The bubbles work like brooms to cleanse the tongue, getting it ready for the next rich mouthful.

Chocolate, Orange and Honey Dessert

I remember making this dessert a long time ago and thought it worthy of a revival. Only cook with chocolate worth eating on its own!

Serves: 4
Preparation time: 10 mins + chilling
Cooking time: 5 mins

100 g (3½ oz) couverture chocolate
300 ml (10 fl oz) fresh cream
1 tablespoon Cointreau
zest of 1 orange
1 teaspoon caster sugar
2 tablespoons honey
2 tablespoons fresh orange juice
1 punnet ripe strawberries

Melt the chocolate in the microwave (5 minutes on 50% power) or over boiling water on the stove. Stir until smooth.

Meanwhile, whip the cream with the Cointreau, orange zest and caster sugar. Fold through the cooled but still melted chocolate, taking care not to blend it too well. When cool it's lovely to come across little chunks of chocolate. Refrigerate.

Warm the honey and blend with the orange juice. To serve, place a mound of chocolate cream in the middle of a plate, surround with ripe strawberries and drizzle with honey and orange juice.

Wine:
Harmonize with the orange notes in the dessert by drinking a Cointreau or Grand Marnier.

Chocolate Blancmange with Saffron Sabayon Sauce

This is the most amazing recipe and combination of flavours. It comes from Michael Cook, the original photographer for my first three cookbooks and is unique—something he reconstructed from the memory of a dish he once ate in northern Italy. The crowning glory is the sauce.

Serves: 6
Preparation time: 15 mins
Cooking time: 7 mins

325 g (11½ oz) good dark chocolate, such as couverture
500 ml (1 pint) milk, plus 1–2 tablespoons extra
1 tablespoon sugar
vanilla extract
1½ tablespoons cornflour

Sauce
2 pinches saffron
½ cup (4 fl oz) sparkling wine
3 egg yolks
50 g (1¾ oz) caster sugar
Almond bread or biscotti to serve

Melt the chocolate in 500 ml (1 pint) milk in the microwave. This is quite simple to do, just heat on HIGH for a couple of minutes and beat. When really hot, add the sugar and a good slosh of vanilla. Dissolve the cornflour in the extra milk and whisk it in. Continue to microwave on HIGH for 2 minutes more, whisking well every 20 seconds. It should by then have boiled. Cook on medium for a further 1 minute to 'cook out' the cornflour. Of course, all of this can be done on the stove top if you prefer.

Pass through a coarse sieve as you pour the mixture into a well-greased or plastic-wrap-lined loaf tin. Cover with more plastic wrap to prevent a skin forming. Cool and refrigerate until set.

To make the sauce, first infuse the saffron in a little of the sparkling wine (a couple of hours is best). Whisk the egg yolks with the sugar until pale and thick. Place bowl over boiling water, whisking until warm and thickened.

Continues over page

Chocolate Blancmange
with Saffron Sabayon Sauce continued

Gradually whisk in the saffron sparkling wine and remaining sparkling wine until the sauce is light and frothy. Put a ladleful of sauce on each plate and then a slice of the chocolate pudding.

Do not serve with cream—almond biscotti or almond bread go well with it.

Cook's note:

If you make this with 70% cocoa fat chocolate, increase the sugar to 2 tablespoons.

Wine:

The chocolate here is not too intense, given the addition of milk and the saffron sauce, so surprisingly it can go with a very rich dessert wine such as a botrytis semillon which picks up the notes of the saffron.

Icy Christmas Pudding

This is a wonderful alternative to a traditional hot Christmas pudding, ideal for warm climates.

Serves: 10
Preparation time: 25 mins + 15 mins standing time + overnight freezing
Cooking time: 2 mins

1 cup Christmas dried and glace fruits of choice, chopped e.g. craisins, raisins, sultanas, glace pineapple, fig, ginger and cherries
¼ cup (2 fl oz) brandy
2 litres (4 pints) good quality vanilla ice-cream, softened
2 cups (10 oz) Vienna almonds, chopped coarsely
360 g (12½ oz) white chocolate, melted
fresh cherries to decorate
icing sugar for dusting

Combine the fruit and brandy in a microwave safe container, cover and heat on high for 2 minutes. Allow to stand for another 15 mins.

Line a 1.75 Litre (3½ pint) pudding basin with plastic wrap, leaving 5cm (2in) or so extending over the edge of the basin.

Combine cooled fruit mixture, softened ice-cream and almonds in a large bowl. Place into the prepared pudding basin. Cover with foil and freeze overnight.

Turn the ice-cream pudding onto a tray, remove the plastic wrap. Measure the outside diameter of the pudding from one side up and over to the other, then return to the freezer.

Lay a sheet of plastic wrap out flat making sure it is bigger than the outside measurement of the pudding—it will probably be about 40cm (16in).

Spread the chocolate in a circle over the plastic wrap. Remove the pudding from the freezer, quickly drape plastic, chocolate-side down, over the pudding. Quickly smooth the pudding with hands. Freeze with the plastic wrap on, for a few minutes or until firm.

Gently peel away plastic and carefully transfer the pudding to a serving plate using a chefs knife and large egg slide. Decorate with cherries if desired and dust with sifted icing sugar.

Wine:
This is rich, but cold and not chocolate dominated, so perhaps an oloroso sherry, vin santo or white port.

Chocolate Macadamia Brownies

Everyone loves chocolate and though these brownies may have begun life as American cookies, the addition of macadamia nuts makes them Australian! Delicious warm from the oven, or cold, if they last that long!

Makes: 18 pieces
Preparation time: 5 mins
Cooking time: 30 mins

125 g (4 oz) butter
100 g (3½ oz) cooking chocolate, broken into pieces
⅔ cup (5 oz) brown sugar
⅓ cup (2¾ oz) plain flour
⅓ cup (1½ oz) good quality cocoa
½ teaspoon baking soda
2 eggs, lightly beaten
100 g (3½ oz) macadamia nuts or pieces

Pre-heat oven to 180°C (350°F, Gas Mark 4). Line the base of an 18 x 28cm (7 x 11in) cake tin with baking paper.

Melt butter, chocolate and brown sugar in a medium sized saucepan over medium heat (or in microwave) and stir frequently until well combined. Remove from heat and simply stir in all the remaining ingredients with a wooden spoon. Pour into the prepared tin and bake for 25–30 minutes or until firm and a knife inserted in the centre comes out cleanly.

Leave in tin to cool a little for 10 minutes and then cut in half lengthwise and then across to make 18 rectangles.

Drink:
Good coffee is the natural partner to these scrumptious morsels.

Chocolate Raspberry Puddings

Chocolate and raspberries are universally popular. Put them together and you have a real winner in this deluxe version of a self-saucing pudding.

Serves: 4
Preparation time: 15 mins
Cooking time: 20 mins

butter or extra light olive oil, to grease
2 tablespoons butter
1/3 cup (2 oz) loosely packed
brown sugar
1 egg
3/4 cup (6 oz) self-raising flour
1 tablespoon Dutch (or other good-quality)
cocoa
1/3 cup (2 3/4 fl oz) milk
2 punnets raspberries
1/3 cup coarsely grated chocolate

Sauce
1/4 cup (2 oz) loosely packed brown sugar
2 teaspoons Dutch (or other good-quality) cocoa
3/4 cup (6 fl oz) boiling water

thick cream, to serve

Preheat oven to moderate, 180°–190°C (350°–375°F, Gas Mark 4). Spray 4 x 1/2 cup (4 fl oz) ramekins with extra light olive oil spray (or grease with butter). Place on a flat baking tray.

Beat butter and sugar together until pale. Add egg and beat again until combined. Add flour, cocoa and milk and stir just until combined. Spoon half into the greased ramekins. Put 5 or 6 raspberries in each and sprinkle over 1 tablespoon chocolate. Top with remaining pudding mixture.

For sauce, mix together sugar and cocoa and sprinkle evenly over each pudding. Pour boiling water gently over the puddings (about 2 tablespoons on each). Bake for about 20 minutes. A skewer inserted in the top may not come out clean because of the sauce that forms underneath so be careful not to overcook. Serve with remaining raspberries and thick cream.

Wine:
Choose a fortified style such as muscat, tokay or even port—chocolate has such an intensity of flavour that it can flatten out dessert wines that don't have the sugar level to stand up to it.

Fudge and Date Slice

Makes: 24 slices
Preparation time: 10 mins
Cooking time: slice 30–35 mins, icing 2 mins

250 g (8 oz) butter
5 tablespoons cocoa
⅓ cup (2¾ fl oz) treacle
1½ cups (11½ oz) brown sugar
1¼ cups (10 oz) self-raising flour
2 eggs, beaten
160 g (5¼ oz) pitted dates, chopped
100 g (3½ oz) pecans, chopped

Icing

60 g (2 oz) dark cooking chocolate, broken
into pieces
3 tablespoons water
1 teaspoon oil
¾ cup (6½ oz) icing sugar, sifted

Pre-heat oven to 180°C (350°F, Gas Mark 4). Line a 25 x 30 x 5cm (10 x 12 x 2in) baking tin with baking paper.

Place butter, cocoa, treacle and brown sugar in saucepan and place over medium low heat, stirring frequently until melted and well combined, around 5 minutes. Cool a little.

Add flour and stir through roughly with a wooden spoon, to make sure mixture is not too hot for the eggs. Add eggs and stir until well combined. Stir through dates and pecans. Pour into baking tin and bake on centre shelf of oven for 20–25 minutes, or until centre feels firm. Cool in tin.

Make icing by combining chocolate, water and oil in a bowl suspended over a saucepan of simmering water. Stir until chocolate has melted and mixture is smooth. Beat in the icing sugar and keep warm. (This can also be done in the microwave.)

Turn fudge out onto a board. Pour icing over, spreading it right to the edge. When set, cut into pieces.

Cook's note:
When spreading any sort of icing it is good to dip the knife into very hot water between strokes. This gives a smoother end result.

Wine:
A good cup of coffee or a fortified wine such as a muscat or port will do the trick here.

Chocolate Soufflé

Serves: 2
Preparation time: 15 minutes
Cooking time: 30 minutes

butter, to grease
1 teaspoon caster sugar
1 teaspoon cocoa
1 tablespoon milk
2 teaspoons cornflour
100 g (3½ oz) dark chocolate, melted
1 egg yolk
2 egg whites
1½ tablespoons caster sugar, extra

Preheat oven to moderately hot 200°C (400°F, Gas Mark 6). Grease two ¾ cup soufflé dishes. Sprinkle base and sides with combined sugar and cocoa; shake off excess.

Combine milk and cornflour and mix well.

Melt chocolate in microwave or double boiler and mix in milk mixture. Remove from heat and beat in egg yolk. Transfer to a large bowl.

Beat egg whites in small bowl with electric mixer until soft peaks form. Gradually beat in extra sugar, one tablespoon at a time, beating to dissolve in between additions. Fold egg white mixture into chocolate mixture, in two batches, until just combined.

Divide soufflé mixture among prepared dishes. Flatten off the top with the back of a knife and run your thumb and forefinger around the rim.

Place on a baking tray and bake in oven about 15 minutes or until soufflés have risen.

Wine:
A sparkling red suits not only the lightness of the soufflés but the richness of the chocolate.

Warm Chocolate Chilli Vincotto Soft-centred Chocolate Puddings

This recipe for wonderful soft-centred puddings was given to me by Luigi Perrone who presented it at one of the wonderful Brisbane Hilton Master Classes. I replicated it on TV and now I share it with you.

Serves: 10
Preparation time: 10 mins
Cooking time: 15 mins

butter, to grease
300 g (10 oz) good quality dark chocolate
300 g (10 oz) butter
8 eggs
1 cup (5 oz) plain flour
⅔ cup (5 oz) sugar
25 g (¾ oz) Calogiuri Vincotto al Peperoncino
vanilla ice-cream, to serve

Preheat oven to 165°C (325°F, Gas Mark 2–3). Grease individual ramekins or dariole moulds with butter.

Melt butter and chocolate in microwave or double saucepan.

Whisk the eggs, flour and sugar together. Add the melted chocolate and the Vincotto al Perperoncino (see Cook's note). Mix well. (At this stage you can refrigerate the mixture for several days—ideal if cooking it for a dinner party. It will take a little longer to cook off baked from cold.)

Pour into the prepared moulds and bake for 10–15 minutes only or until just firm. Serve immediately with ice-cream.

Wine:

There are two things to consider here, the rich dark chocolate and the subtle chilli hit, so the rich, spicy flavours of a sparkling shiraz are perfect.

Cook's note:

Vincotto is made by cooking the must of grapes which have withered on the vine for 30 days beyond ripening. After cooking, it is aged in oak casks. Vincotto al Perperoncino has an added hit from hot peppers. If you can't get vincotto, use some liqueur instead.

Chocolate Self-Saucing Pudding

This is a very simple version of an old favourite—and just as easy as the packet ones you can buy!
Don't be dismayed at how it looks coming out of the oven—the thick, rich sauce is underneath it.

Serves :4–6
Preparation time: 5–10 mins
Cooking time: 35 mins

Pudding

1 cup (5 oz) self-raising flour
100 g (3½ oz) brown sugar
⅓ cup (1¼ oz) good quality cocoa
2 tablespoons (1½ oz) melted butter
½ cup (4 fl oz) milk

Sauce

¼ cup (¾ oz) cocoa
¾ cup (5¾ oz) brown sugar
380 ml (13 oz) boiling water

vanilla ice-cream, to serve

Pre-heat oven to 180°C (350°F, Gas Mark 4).

Sift dry pudding ingredients straight into oven-proof pudding basin e.g. 2 litre (4 pint) soufflé dish. Combine melted butter and milk and stir in until well combined.

Mix cocoa and brown sugar and sprinkle over pudding batter. Gently pour boiling water on top of this by pouring it over the back of a spoon to avoid disturbing the chocolate batter too much. Immediately bake pudding in moderate oven for 35 minutes. Allow to stand a couple of minutes only before serving. The longer it stands, the more the sauce will be absorbed into the pudding.

Dig deep to scoop out the pudding as at the bottom will be the thick sauce. Serve in a bowl beside some vanilla ice-cream.

Cook's note:

These can be made as individual puddings. simply distribute the pudding batter evenly between six greased ½ cup ramekins or soufflé dishes, sprinkle over the topping and pour over boiling water and bake for 15–20 minutes.

Wine:

Chocolate has such an intensity of flavours that it flattens out dessert wines. Choose instead a liqueured tokay or muscat or even your favourite port.

Chocolate Truffles

Forget everything you've heard about not making chocolates in summer. These are fine made then or at any time of year.

Makes: 30 truffles
Preparation time: 10 mins
Cooking time: 5 mins

1 ¼ cups (10 fl oz) cream
155–220 g (5–7 oz) dark couverture chocolate (not compound)
1–2 tablespoons liqueur, e.g. Cointreau, Grand Marnier
cocoa, for dusting (optional)

Bring cream to the boil and simmer until thick and bubbly and reduced by about half. Melt chocolate in the microwave, or over hot water in a double boiler, and stir into cream until smooth. Stir in liqueur to flavour. Cool, stirring occasionally, until thick enough to pipe. Using a piping bag, pipe chocolate mixture into rosettes in paper cases and dust with cocoa, if desired. Refrigerate before serving.

Cook's note:
Remember, better quality chocolate makes better truffles, but how much chocolate you use is up to you. More chocolate will make a firmer truffle; less will make a soft truffle that needs longer refrigeration.

Wine:
With chocolate, choose a liqueur muscat or tokay, a particular specialty of Rutherglen, but also made in other areas of Australia. Alternatively, serve with port or good coffee.

Chocolate Sauce

Everyone needs a good, basic chocolate sauce recipe. This is mine!

Makes: nearly 2 cups
Preparation: 5 mins
Cooking: 5 mins

60 g (2 oz) butter, chopped
⅔ cup (5½ fl oz) cream
200 g (8 oz) dark eating quality chocolate, chopped
2 tablespoons liqueur e.g. Tia Maria or espresso coffee

Combine butter and cream in a small saucepan and stir over low heat until butter is melted. Stir in chocolate and continue to stir until smooth. Stir in liqueur.

Use over ice-cream, crepes, waffles, pancakes or whatever you wish.

Cook's note:

The microwave is ideal for melting chocolate. The sauce can be completely made by melting in a microwave safe container and stirring occasionally.

WEIGHTS & MEASUREMENTS

Oven Temperatures

100°C	very slow	200°F	Gas Mark 1
120°C	very slow	250°F	Gas Mark 1
150°C	slow	300°F	Gas Mark 2
165°C	warm	325°F	Gas Mark 2–3
180°C	moderate	350°F	Gas Mark 4
190°C	moderately hot	375°F	Gas Mark 5
200°C	moderately hot	400°F	Gas Mark 6
220°C	hot	420°F	Gas Mark 7
230°C	very hot	450°F	Gas Mark 8
250°C	very hot	485°F	Gas Mark 9

For fan-forced ovens reduce recommended temperature by 20°C

Solid Measures

Metric	Imperial
10 g	1/3 oz
15 g	1/2 oz
20 g	2/3 oz
30 g	1 oz
45 g	1 1/2 oz
60 g	2 oz
100 g	3 1/2 oz
125 g	4 oz
150 g	5 oz
165 g	5 1/2 oz
180 g	6 oz
200 g	7 oz
250 g	8 oz
300 g	10 oz
350 g	11 1/2 oz
400 g	13 oz
500 g	1 lb
750 g	1 1/2 lb
1 kg	2 lb

Fluid Measures

Metric	Imperial	Standard Cups
5 ml		1 teaspoon
20 ml	1 fl oz	1 tablespoon
15 ml		1 tablespoon (NZ and US)
50 ml	1 3/4 fl oz	
60 ml	2 fl oz	1/4 cup
80 ml	2 3/4 fl oz	1/3 cup
100 ml	3 1/2 fl oz	
125 ml	4 fl oz	1/2 cup
150 ml	5 fl oz	2/3 cup
200 ml	6 1/2 fl oz	
250 ml	8 fl oz	1 cup
500 ml	16 fl oz	2 cups
750 ml	24 fl oz	3 cups
1 L	32 fl oz	4 cups

INDEX

A

almonds
    Baked Quinces with Almond Tuiles 225
    Chocolate Almond Meringue Cake 240
anchovies
    Anchovy Sauce 182
    Rocket and Anchovy Butter 154
    Tuna with Anchovy Sauce 139
Apple Cake, Caramelised 214
Aromatic Vegetables 68
Asian-Scented Broth with Chicken Wontons 107
Asian-Style Roast Pork Salad 189
Asparagus on Garlicky Bean Puree
    with Crisp Pancetta 72

B

Baby Octopus, Marinated 135
Baked Coconut Custard with Mango 211
Baked Quinces with Almond Tuiles 225
Bean Curd, Deep-fried, with Chilli Sauce 118
Beef and Udon Noodle Soup 111
berry
    Berry Brulée 218
    Berry Purée 230
Bloody Mary Oyster Shooters 33
bread and butter pudding
    Chocolate 239
    Orange 207
Bream, Grilled, with Cumin 143
Brioche, Mushrooms En 87
Brownies, Chocolate Macadamia 253

C

cake(s)
    Caramelised Apple Cake 214
    Chocolate Almond Meringue Cake 240
    Lemon Polenta Cake with Lemon Mascarpone
        204
    Simple Chocolate Fudge Cake 241
Caramelised Apple Cake 214
Cataplana 127
Celeriac Puree 182
Cheat's Berry Brulée 218
chicken

Asian-Scented Broth with Chicken Wontons 107
Chicken and Sweetcorn Soup 103
Chicken Breasts with Red Capsicum Aïoli 157
Chicken Consommé with Angel Hair 104
Chicken in a Pot with Preserved Lemon 158
Chicken in a Salt Crust 161
Chicken Kofta 100
Grilled Thai Chicken 145
Mustard-crusted Chicken Breast with Fennel and
    Orange 162
Pasta with Chicken Livers, Sage and Rocket 166
chilli
    Chilli Sauce 118
    Pasta with Prawns and Chilli Oil 125
    Whole Thai-style Steamed Fish with Chilli,
        Garlic and Coriander 153
Chinese Roast Duck Salad 197
chocolate
    Chocolate Almond Meringue Cake 240
    Chocolate Beignets 236
    Chocolate Blacmange with Saffron Sabayon
        Sauce 248
    Chocolate Bread and Butter Pudding 239
    Chocolate Crème Brulée 242
    Chocolate Ganache Tart 245
    Chocolate, Orange and Honey Dessert 247
    Chocolate Raspberry Puddings 254
    Chocolate Sauce 266
    Chocolate Self-Saucing Pudding 262
    Chocolate Soufflé 258
    Chocolate Truffles 265
    Simple Chocolate Fudge Cake 241
    Warm Chocolate Chilli Vincotto Soft-centred
        Chocolate Puddings 261
Christmas Pudding, Icy 251
Clams, Portugese-style 128
coconut
    Baked Coconut Custard with Mango 211
    Pumpkin and Coconut Soup 79
Coeur à la Crème 230
coriander
    Duck Soup with Coriander and Noodles 108
    Whole Thai-style Steamed Fish with Chilli,
        Garlic and Coriander 153

corn
    Chicken and Sweetcorn Soup 103
Corned Beef with Horseradish Cream
    and Olive Mash 196
couscous 150
    Couscous Salad 185
Crab and Lemon, Spirelli with 99
Crème Brulée, Chocolate 242
curries
    Quick Fish Curry 144
    Thai-style Red Curry of Duck Livers 165

D

Date and Fudge Slice 257
Deep-fried Bean Curd with Chilli Sauce 118
Dry Portugese Prawn Soup 88
duck
    Chinese Roast Duck Salad 197
    Duck Soup with Coriander and Noodles 108
    Thai-style Red Curry of Duck Livers 165

F

figs
    Figs in Prosciutto 21
    Honeyed Figs 229
fish
    Fish Balls with Lemon Grass 38
    Fish with Chermoula Marinade
        and Couscous 150
    Fish with Rocket and Anchovy Butter 154
    Grilled Bream with Cumin 143
    Quick Fish Curry 144
    Whole Baby Snapper with Tomato
        and Lime Salsa 149
    Whole Thai-style Steamed Fish with Chilli,
        Garlic and Coriander 153
Fritters, Eggplant and Zucchini 18
Fruit, Gratinéed 226
Fruit Salad, Warm Winter 213
fudge
    Fudge and Date Slice 257
    Simple Chocolate Fudge Cake 241

G

Ganache Tart, Chocolate 245
garlicky bean purée
  Asparagus on Garlicky Bean Puree
    with Crisp Pancetta 72
  Lamb Mini-roast with Garlicky White
    Bean Purée 178
Gazpacho, Real Spanish 114
Glass Noodle Salad 122
Gnocchi with Pumpkin, Horseradish
  and Spinach 121
Green Pawpaw Salad 71
Grilled Bream with Cumin 143
Grilled Thai Chicken 145
Grilled Veal Cutlet with Tomato Alioli 181

H

Honeyed Figs 229

I

Icy Christmas Pudding 251

K

Kangaroo Fillet, Seared, in a Salad
  with Moroccan Flavours 185

L

Labna 29
Laksa 124
lamb
  Lamb Chinese Style 177
  Lamb Mini-roast with Garlicky White
    Bean Purée 178
  Moroccan Lamb Kofta on Rosemary Skewers 173
  Moroccan Lamb Shanks with Quinces 174
lemon
  Chicken in a Pot with Preserved Lemon 158
  Lemon or Lime Tart 203
  Lemon Polenta Cake with Lemon
    Mascarpone 204
  Spirelli with Crab and Lemon 99
lemon grass
  Fish Balls with Lemon Grass 38
  Prawns Poached in Lemon Grass Broth 91
Lettuce Leaves, Thai Salad Wrapped in 53
Little Round Sandwiches 30
liver
  Pasta with Chicken Livers, Sage and Rocket 166

Thai-style Red Curry of Duck Livers 165

M

macadamia nuts
  Chocolate Macadamia Brownies 253
  Spiced Macadamia Nuts 25
marinade(s) 170
  Chermoula Marinade 150
Marinated Baby Octopus 135
Mascarpone, Lemon 204
Michael's Mushroom Risotto 83
Modern Salad Niçoise 136
Moroccan Lamb Kofta on Rosemary Skewers 173
Moroccan Lamb Shanks with Quinces 174
mushrooms
  Fennel and Mushroom Salad 112
  Michael's Mushroom Risotto 83
  Mushrooms En Brioche 87
  Wild Mushroom Pasta 84
Mustard-crusted Chicken Breast with Fennel
  and Orange 162

N

Nam Jim 170
noodles
  Beef and Udon Noodle Soup 111
  Duck Soup with Coriander and Noodles 108
  Glass Noodle Salad 122
  Spicy Pork Stir-Fry with Noodles 194
Nori Rolls and Smoked Salmon 46

O

Octopus, Marinated Baby 135
orange(s)
  Chocolate, Orange and Honey Dessert 247
  Mustard-crusted Chicken Breast with Fennel
    and Orange 162
  Orange Bread and Butter Pudding 207
  Oranges with Honey and Olive Oil 13
  Roasted Tomato and Orange Soup 80
Oysters with Different Toppings 34

P

Pad Thai 193
Paella, Seafood 132
Passionfruit Butter Tarts 200
pasta
  Chicken Consommé with Angel Hair 104

Pasta Shells with Tomato, Basil and Tapenade 65
Pasta with Chicken Livers, Sage and Rocket 166
Pasta with Prawns and Chilli Oil 125
Seafood Ravioli 95
Spirelli with Crab and Lemon 99
Wild Mushroom Pasta 84
Pastry 203, 245
  Sweet Shortcrust Pastry 200
Pawpaw (Green) Salad 71
Pea and Lettuce Soup 75
Peaches, Poached 208
pears
  Pear Confit 10
  Pear Vichyssoise with Spinach 76
pesto
  Mint Pesto 54
  Pistachio and Parsley Pesto 190
Pistachio and Parsley Pesto 190
Plum Clafoutis 221
Poached Peaches 208
Polenta Canapés with Prawns 49
pork
  Asian-Style Roast Pork Salad 189
  Pork Dim Sims 62
  Pork Fillet with Pistachio and Parsley Pesto 190
  Spicy Pork Stir-Fry with Noodles 194
Portugese-style Clams 128
Potato Roesti with Seared Beef and Wasabi 57
prawns
  Dry Portugese Prawn Soup 88
  Pasta with Prawns and Chilli Oil 125
  Polenta Canapés with Prawns 49
  Prawn Risotto with Saffron 131
  Prawn Soup 92
  Prawns Poached in Lemon Grass Broth 91
  Spicy Thai Prawns 96
proscuitto
  Figs in Prosciutto 21
  Spaghetti with Prosciutto and Rocket 186
pumpkin
  Gnocchi with Pumpkin, Horseradish
    and Spinach 121
  Pumpkin and Coconut Soup 79
  Pumpkin Puree 169

Q

Quail, Spiced, with Nam Jim 170
Quick Fish Curry 144

quinces
    Baked Quinces with Almond Tuiles 225
    Moroccan Lamb Shanks with Quinces 174

R
Ravioli, Seafood 95
Real Spanish Gazpacho 114
Red Capsicum Aïoli 157
Rhubarb Tarte Tatin 222
Rice Paper Rolls 58
Ricotta Balls 26
risotto
    Michael's Mushroom Risotto 83
    Prawn Risotto with Saffron 131
roasted tomato
    Roasted Tomato and Orange Soup 80
    Roasted Tomato and Spring Onion Salad 113

S
Saffron Sabayon Sauce 248
salads
    Asian-Style Roast Pork Salad 189
    Chinese Roast Duck Salad 197
    Couscous Salad 185
    Fennel and Mushroom Salad 112
    Glass Noodle Salad 122
    Green Pawpaw Salad 71
    Modern Salad Niçoise 136
    Roasted Tomato and Spring Onion Salad 113
    Thai Salad Wrapped in Lettuce Leaves 53
salmon
    Smoked Salmon and Nori Rolls 46
    Spring Salmon 146
San Choy Bau, Easy 61
Sandwiches, Little Round 30
sauces
    Anchovy Sauce 139, 182
    Chilli Sauce 118
    Chocolate 266
    Saffron Sabayon Sauce 248
    Yoghurt Sauce 173
Scallops on the Shell with Asian-Style Vinaigrette 41
Scallops Steamed with Ginger, Shallots
  and Sesame 37
seafood
    Seafood Noodle Balls 45
    Seafood Paella 132
    Seafood Ravioli 95

Seared Kangaroo Fillet in a Salad
  with Moroccan Flavours 185
Self-Saucing Pudding, Chocolate 262
Shortcrust Pastry, Sweet 200
Simple Chocolate Fudge Cake 241
Smoked Salmon and Nori Rolls 46
Soufflé, Chocolate 258
soups
    Asian-Scented Broth with Chicken Wontons 107
    Beef and Udon Noodle Soup 111
    Chicken and Sweetcorn Soup 103
    Chicken Consommé with Angel Hair 104
    Chilled Minted Pea and Lettuce Soup 75
    Dry Portugese Prawn Soup 88
    Duck Soup with Coriander and Noodles 108
    Pear Vichyssoise with Spinach 76
    Prawn Soup 92
    Pumpkin and Coconut Soup 79
    Real Spanish Gazpacho 114
    Roasted Tomato and Orange Soup 80
Spaghetti with Prosciutto and Rocket 186
Spatchcock Dijonnaise 169
Spiced Macadamia Nuts 25
Spiced Quail with Nam Jim 170
Spicy Pork Stir-Fry with Noodles 194
Spicy Thai Prawns 96
spinach
    Gnocchi with Pumpkin, Horseradish
      and Spinach 121
    Pear Vichyssoise with Spinach 76
Spirelli with Crab and Lemon 99
Spring Salmon 146
Sticky Toffee Pudding 233
stir-fries
    Spicy Pork Stir-Fry with Noodles 194
Stone-Fruit Galette 210
Summer Pudding 217

T
Tapenade 22
    Pasta Shells with Tomato, Basil and Tapenade 65
    Tomato Tarts with Fetta and Tapenade 17
tarts
    Chocolate Ganache Tart 245
    Lemon or Lime Tart 203
    Tiny Passionfruit Butter Tarts 200
Thai Chicken Balls 50
Thai food

Grilled Thai Chicken 145
Pad Thai 193
Spicy Thai Prawns 96
Thai Chicken Balls 50
Thai Salad Wrapped in Lettuce Leaves 53
Thai-style Red Curry of Duck Livers 165
Whole Thai-style Steamed Fish with Chilli,
  Garlic and Coriander 153
Thai Salad Wrapped in Lettuce Leaves 53
Thai-style Red Curry of Duck Livers 165
Tiny Passionfruit Butter Tarts 200
Toffee Pudding, Sticky 233
tomato
    Grilled Veal Cutlet with Tomato Alioli 181
    Pasta Shells with Tomato, Basil and Tapenade 65
    Roasted Tomato and Orange Soup 80
    Roasted Tomato and Spring Onion Salad 113
    Tomato and Lime Salsa 149
    Tomato Tarts with Fetta and Tapenade 17
Truffles, Chocolate 265
tuna
    Tuna with Anchovy Sauce 139
    Tuna with Wasabi and Fresh Herb Butter 140

V
Veal Cutlets, Grilled, with Tomato Alioli 181
Vegetables, Aromatic 68

W
Warm Chocolate Chilli Vincotto Soft-centred
  Chocolate Puddings 261
Warm Winter Fruit Salad 213
wasabi
    Potato Roesti with Seared Beef and Wasabi 57
    Tuna with Wasabi and Fresh Herb Butter 140
Watermelon with Iced Gin 14
Whole Baby Snapper with Tomato
  and Lime Salsa 149
Whole Thai-style Steamed Fish with Chilli,
  Garlic and Coriander 153
Wild Mushroom Pasta 84

Y
Yoghurt Sauce 173

Z
Zucchini and Eggplant Fritters 18

First published in Australia in 2009 by
New Holland Publishers (Australia) Pty Ltd
Sydney • Auckland • London • Cape Town

This paperback edition published in 2013
1/66 Gibbes Street, Chatswood NSW 2067 Australia
218 Lake Road Northcote Auckland 0746 New Zealand
The Chandlery Unit 114 50 Westminster Bridge Road London SE17QY United Kingdom
Wembly Square First Floor Solan Road Gardens Cape Town 8001 South Africa
www.newhollandpublishers.com

National Library of Australia Cataloguing-in-Publication-Data:

Author:	Milan, Lyndey.
Title:	Lyndey Milan the best collection : fast, fabulous food / Lyndey Milan.
ISBN:	9781741108934 (hbk.)
	9781742574639 (pbk.)
Notes:	Includes index.
Subjects:	Quick and easy cookery.
	Cookery.
Dewey Number:	641.5

Publisher: Fiona Schultz
Publishing Manager: Lliane Clarke
Junior Editor: Ashlea Wallington
Designer: Hayley Norman
Photography: Michael Cook, Joe Filshie and Graeme Gillies for New Holland Publishers.
Proofreader: Bronwyn Phillips
Chef and Styling: Lyndey Milan
Assistant Chef: Andrew Ballard pp 19, 24, 26 ,31, 32, 51, 55, 59, 64, 74, 75, 81, 82, 89, 90, 93, 98,
102, 105, 109, 110, 115, 119, 120, 130, 138, 142, 147, 152, 156, 159, 164, 175, 176, 178,
180,183, 184, 195, 202, 206, 212, 219, 228, 238, 243, 244, 249, 251, 252, 256, 259, 266, 263,
264, 265.
Styling: Georgina Dolling pp 28, 39, 43, 44, 52, 101, 160, 172, 209, 237.
Assistant: Ishbel Thorpe
Production Manager: Olga Dementiev
Printer: Toppan Leefung Printing Ltd (China)

10 9 8 7 6 5 4 3 2 1